MW00386609

Small Wall Quilts

LEISURE ARTS®

CREATED FOR LEISURE ARTS BY HOUSE OF WHITE BIRCHES

Contents

SMALL WALL QUILTS © 2003, 2001, 2000, 1999, 1998, 1997 House of White Birches, 306 East Parr Road, Berne, IN 46711, (260) 589-4000. Customer_Service@ whitebirches.com. Made in USA.

All rights reserved. This publication is protected under federal copyright laws. Reproduction or distribution of this publication or any other House of White Birches publication, including publications which are out of print, is prohibited unless specifically authorized. This includes, but is not limited to, any form of reproduction or distribution on or through the Internet, including posting, scanning or e-mail transmission.

We have made every effort to ensure that the instructions in this book are complete and accurate. We cannot be responsible for human error, typographical mistakes or variations in individual work.

The designs in this book are protected by copyright; however, you may make the designs for your personal use. This right is surpassed when the designs are made by employees or sold commercially.

ISBN: 1-57486-356-8

CREDITS: Anniversary Florals, page 22, provided by DMC, French Country, page 110, provided by Coats & Clark.

Introduction

In the early days of quilting, women quilted with one primary purpose in mind—to make cozy bed covers for their families. The skilled quilter made full use of the fabrics she had available to make a beautiful quilt, but her primary goal was stitching a warm, durable bed cover.

Princess Star

Quilting has evolved through the years, and our grandmothers would look enviously at our many choices. Today we're making quilts of all sizes, with glorious fabrics and an ever-growing array

Fiery Baskets

of patterns. We now use quilts to decorate walls in every room, in addition to making cozy bed covers. Because of their small size and today's quick-and-easy techniques, speedy quilters sometimes complete a gorgeous wall quilt in just a weekend.

In this book you'll find a stunning collection of wall quilts. Your most difficult decision will be "Which one should I make first?"

For a contemporary look, try the creative quilts on pages 52 and 86. Both quilts have an artistic quality worthy of display in a museum.

If your home has a cottage look, you'll love quilting with lovely floral fabrics such as those found in Anniversary Florals on page 22 and China Blue Basket on page 41. It only takes a change in color to make this quilt enhance the decor of any kitchen.

Chocolate Chips

Made in shades of chocolate prints, Chocolate Chips on page 16 combines two blocks, the Ohio Star and Thrifty, to create a unique design. Wall quilts are a wonderful way for you to try out new quilt blocks. You'll find your options are unlimited. When it gets right down to it, these wall quilts are just plain fun to make!

Savannah Star

BY LUCY A. FAZELY

Celebrate those "star" occasions with this star quilt made with five different half-square Log Cabin blocks that create the star design. Although the designer of this quilt chose to honor the city of Savannah, this star quilt could occupy a place of honor in any city in the world.

Savannah Star

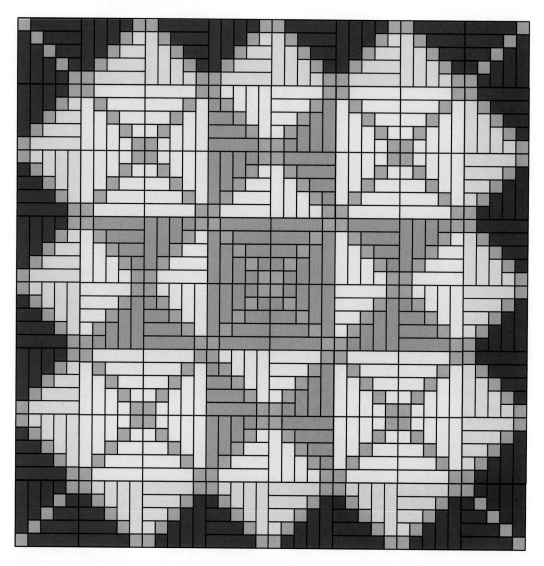

Savannah Star
Placement Diagram
40" x 40"

Savannah Star

Project Specifications

Quilt Size: 40" x 40"

Block Size: 5" x 5"

Number of Blocks: 64

Fabric & Batting

- ⅜ yard light floral print
- ½ yard each mauve and blue prints
- ⅔ yard gold print
- 1 yard off-white print
- Backing 44" x 44"
- Batting 44" x 44"
- 5 yards self-made or purchased binding

Supplies & Tools

- Neutral color all-purpose thread
- Basic sewing tools and supplies, rotary cutter, ruler and cutting mat

Instructions

1. Cut the following fabric width strips from off-white print: eleven 1½" and one each 2½", 3½" and 4½".

2. Cut the following fabric width strips from mauve print: three 1½" and one each 2½", 3½" and 4½".

3. Cut 15 strips gold print 1½" by fabric width.

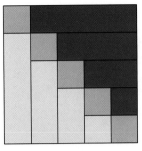

Savannah Star
5" x 5" Block
Make 24

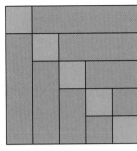

Savannah Star
5" x 5" Block
Make 4

Savannah Star
5" x 5" Block
Make 4

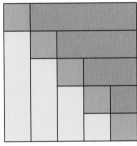

Savannah Star
5" x 5" Block
Make 16

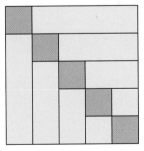

Savannah Star
5" x 5" Block
Make 16

4. Cut eight strips light floral print 1½" by fabric width.

5. Cut the following fabric width strips from blue print: four 1½" and one each 2½", 3½" and 4½".

Savannah Star

6. Sew a 1½" gold print strip to each of the following referring to Figure 1 which shows only the mauve/gold versions: two each 1½" off-white and blue prints; one each 1½" mauve and light floral prints; and all of the 2½", 3½" and 4½" strips. Press all seams toward the gold print strip.

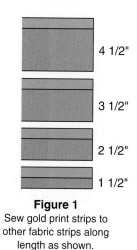

4 1/2"

3 1/2"

2 1/2"

1 1/2"

Figure 1
Sew gold print strips to
other fabric strips along
length as shown.

7. Subcut 1½"/1½" strip sets in 1½" segments referring to Figure 2 for color combinations and number of segments needed. Subcut remaining strip sets in 1½" segments referring to Figure 3 which shows only the mauve/gold versions.

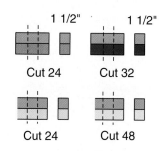

1 1/2"   1 1/2"

Cut 24   Cut 32

Cut 24   Cut 48

Figure 2
Cut 1 1/2"/1 1/2" strip sets as shown.

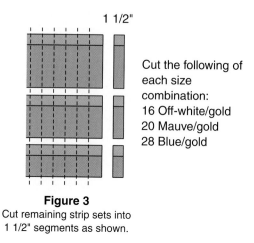

1 1/2"

Cut the following of
each size
combination:
16 Off-white/gold
20 Mauve/gold
28 Blue/gold

Figure 3
Cut remaining strip sets into
1 1/2" segments as shown.

8. Sew segments together as shown in Figure 4 to make Four-Patch units.

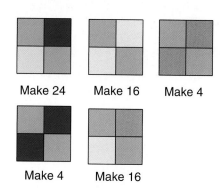

Make 24   Make 16   Make 4

Make 4   Make 16

Figure 4
Join segments to make Four-Patch units as shown.

9. Sew mauve/off-white and off-white/off-white Four-Patch units to 1½"-wide off-white strips as shown in Figure 5. Press seams toward the off-white strip; cut strip even with segments as shown in Figure 6.

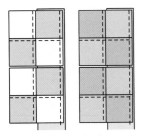
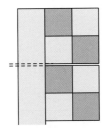

Figure 5
Sew Four-Patch units
to 1 1/2"-wide off-white
print strips.

Figure 6
Cut strip even
with Four-Patch
units as shown.

10. Repeat with mauve/mauve Four-Patch units and a mauve print 1½" strip, light floral/blue units with two light floral print 1½" strips and blue/blue units with a blue print 1½" strip, again referring to Figure 6.

11. Continue adding segments to pieced units and sewing units to 1½" strips, matching segment and strip colors to make blocks referring to Figure 7.

12. Arrange pieced blocks in rows referring to the Placement Diagram for positioning of blocks. Join blocks in rows; join rows to complete pieced center.

13. Sandwich batting between completed top and prepared backing piece. Pin or baste layers together to hold flat.

14. Quilt as desired by hand or machine. When quilting is complete, remove pins or basting; trim edges even.

15. Bind edges with self-made or purchased binding to finish. ❖

Make 24

Make 4

Make 4

Make 16

Make 16

Figure 7
Continue adding segments and
stitching to strips and trimming to
make blocks as shown.

Miniature Variable Star Puzzle

BY CHRISTINE CARLSON

Thinking it would be a real puzzle to pick out all of the different Variable Star blocks in the quilt, the quiltmaker titled this quilt Miniature Variable Star Puzzle. You don't, however, have to be able to solve puzzles to appreciate this charming little quilt. With these quick-piecing techniques, you'll be stumping people who won't be able to figure out how you were able to make this quilt so quickly.

Miniature Variable Star Puzzle

2 1/4" x 15 3/4"

2 1/4" x 16 1/4"

Miniature Variable Star Puzzle
Placement Diagram
15 3/4" x 20 3/4"
(includes binding)

Miniature Variable Star Puzzle

Project Specifications

Quilt Size: 15¾" x 20¾" (includes binding)
Unit Size: 1¼" x 1¼"
Number of Units: 58

Fabric & Batting

- 8" x 18" rectangle bright blue print
- Fat quarter light blue print
- ½ yard medium blue floral print
- Backing 19" x 24"
- Batting 19" x 24"
- 2⅜ yards self-made or purchased binding

Supplies & Tools

- Neutral color all-purpose thread
- White quilting thread
- Basic sewing tools and supplies

Instructions

1. Cut two strips 1¾" x 18" from 8" x 18" rectangle bright blue print. Cut strips into 1¾" square segments for A. You will need 18 A squares.

2. Cut one strip 2½" x 18" from the remainder of the 8" x 18" rectangle bright blue print. Cut strip into 2½" square segments for B; you will need six B squares.

3. Cut two strips 1¾" x 22" light blue print. Cut strips into 1¾" square segments for C; you will need 24 C squares.

4. Cut four strips 2½" x 22" from the remainder of the light blue print. Cut strips into 2½" square segments for D; you will need 29 D squares.

5. Cut one strip 1¾" by fabric width medium blue floral print. Cut strip into 1¾" square segments for E; you will need 17 E squares.

6. Cut two strips 2½" by fabric width medium blue floral print. Cut strips into 2½" square segments for F; you will need 23 F squares.

7. Stack several B, D and F squares with wrong sides together; cut each square stack in half on both diagonals as shown in Figure 1 to make 24 B, 116 D and 92 F triangles.

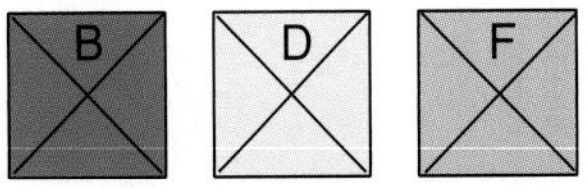

Figure 1
Cut B, D and F squares
in half on both diagonals.

Miniature Variable Star Puzzle

8. Join one B and D triangle to make a B-D unit as shown in Figure 2; repeat for 24 B-D units.

Figure 2
Join 1 B and D
triangle to make
a B-D unit.

9. Join two B-D units as shown in Figure 3; repeat for 12 B-D square units.

Figure 3
Join 2 B-D units
as shown.

10. Repeat steps 8 and 9 with D and F triangles to make 46 D-F square units.

11. Arrange the B-D units with the D-F units and the A, C and E squares in rows referring to Figure 4; join squares in rows.

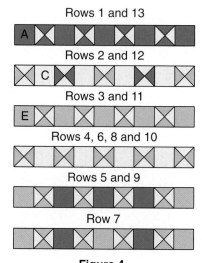

Figure 4
Arrange the B-D units with the
D-F units and the A, C and E
squares in rows.

12. Arrange the rows referring to Figure 5; join rows to complete the pieced center. Press seams in one direction.

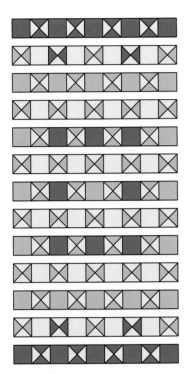

Figure 5
Arrange the rows as shown.

13. Cut two strips each 2½" x 16¾" and 2½" x 15¾" medium blue floral print.

14. Sew the longer strips to opposite long sides and shorter strips to the top and bottom; press seams toward strips.

15. Sandwich batting between completed top and prepared backing; pin or baste layers together to hold flat.

16. Hand-quilt in the ditch of seams and in diagonal lines ½" apart on border strips using white quilting thread.

17. When quilting is complete, trim edges even; remove pins or basting.

18. Bind edges with self-made or purchased binding to finish. ❖

Chocolate Chips

BY JANET JONES WORLEY

Made in shades of chocolate prints, this quilt certainly looks like delicious chocolate chip cookies are marching across it. Two blocks, the Ohio Star and Thrifty, combine to create the interesting design. Using these quick-piecing methods, this small quilt could almost be finished before the cookies have come out of the oven.

Chocolate Chips

Project Specifications

Quilt Size: 45" x 54"

Block Size: 9" x 9"

Number of Blocks: 12

Fabric & Batting

- ⅛ yard light teal print
- ¼ yard small floral print
- ½ yard beige print
- ⅝ yard each chocolate and yellow prints
- 1¼ yards dark teal floral
- Backing 49" x 58"
- Batting 49" x 58"
- 6 yards self-made or purchased binding

Supplies & Tools

- Neutral color all-purpose thread
- Clear nylon monofilament
- Basic sewing tools and supplies, rotary cutter, ruler and cutting mat

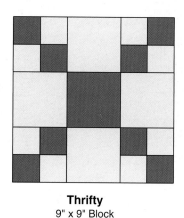

Thrifty
9" x 9" Block

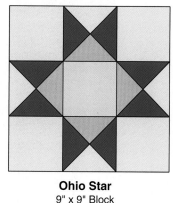

Ohio Star
9" x 9" Block

Making Thrifty Blocks

1. Cut three strips each 2" by fabric width chocolate and beige prints. Sew a chocolate print strip to a beige print strip with right sides together along length; repeat for three strip sets. Press seams toward darkest fabrics.

2. Subcut strip sets into 2" segments; you will need 48 segments.

3. Join two segments to make a Four-Patch unit as

Chocolate Chips

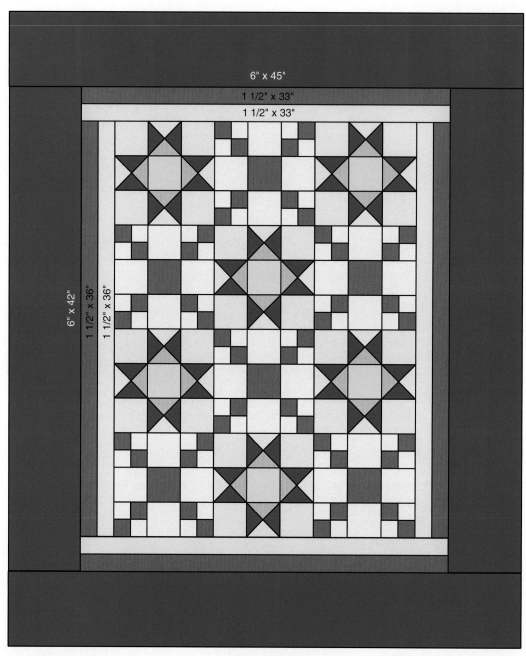

6" x 45"

1 1/2" x 33"

1 1/2" x 33"

6" x 42"

1 1/2" x 36"

1 1/2" x 36"

Chocolate Chips
Placement Diagram
45" x 54"

shown in Figure 1; repeat for 24 units.

Figure 1
Join 2 segments to make
a Four-Patch unit.

4. Cut two strips beige print 3½" by fabric width. Subcut strips into 3½" square units; you will need 24 beige print squares.

5. Cut one strip chocolate print 3½" by fabric width. Subcut strip into 3½" square units; you will need 12 chocolate print squares.

6. Arrange four beige print squares and one chocolate print square with four Four-Patch units as shown in Figure 2. Join units in rows; join rows to complete one block. Repeat for six Thrifty blocks.

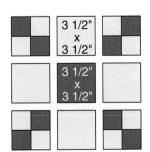

Figure 2
Arrange 4 beige print squares
and 1 chocolate print square
with 4 Four-Patch units; join
to make a Thrifty block.

Making Ohio Star Blocks

1. Cut one strip light teal print 3½" by fabric width; subcut into 3½" square units. You will need six light teal print squares.

2. Cut two strips yellow print 3½" by fabric width; subcut into 3½" square units. You will need 24 yellow print squares.

3. Cut two strips dark teal floral and one strip each yellow and small floral prints 4¼" by fabric width. Subcut each strip into 4¼" square segments. You will need 12 dark teal floral and six each yellow and small floral print squares.

4. Draw two diagonal lines on the wrong side of each yellow print and small floral print square as shown in Figure 3.

Figure 3
Draw 2 diagonal lines on
the wrong side of each
yellow print and small
floral print square.

5. Layer a dark teal floral square right sides together with each marked square. Sew a ¼" seam on

Chocolate Chips

each side of one marked line as shown in Figure 4.

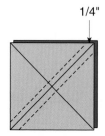

Figure 4
Sew a 1/4" seam on each
side of 1 marked line.

6. Cut stitched unit apart on the remaining unstitched diagonal as shown in Figure 5.

Figure 5
Cut stitched unit apart on the
remaining unstitched diagonal.

7. Cut resulting triangles on the line between the stitched lines to make four triangle units as shown in Figure 6. Repeat for all marked squares.

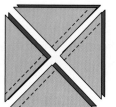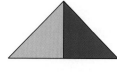

Figure 6
Cut resulting triangles on line between
stitched lines to make 4 triangle units.

8. Join a teal/yellow triangle unit with a teal/small floral triangle unit as shown in Figure 7; repeat for 24 units.

Figure 7
Join a teal/yellow triangle
unit with a teal/small floral
triangle unit.

9. Join two yellow print squares with a triangle unit to make a row as shown in Figure 8; repeat. Join two triangle units with a teal print square to make a row as shown in Figure 9.

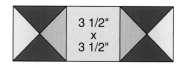

Figure 8
Join 2 yellow print squares with
a triangle unit to make a row.

Figure 9
Join 2 triangle units with a light
teal print square to make a row.

10. Join the rows to complete one Ohio Star block as shown in Figure 10; repeat for six blocks.

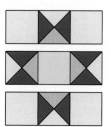

Figure 10
Join the rows to complete
1 Ohio Star block.

11. Join two Thrifty blocks with one Ohio Star block to make a row; repeat for two rows. Press seams in one direction.

12. Join two Ohio Star blocks with one Thrifty block to make a row; repeat for two rows. Press seams in one direction.

13. Join rows to complete pieced center referring to the Placement Diagram for positioning of rows; press seams in one direction.

Finishing Quilt

1. Cut two strips each 2" x 36½" yellow and chocolate prints. Sew a yellow print strip to a chocolate print strip with right sides together along length; press seams toward chocolate print strips. Repeat for two strips.

2. Sew a pieced strip to opposite long sides of the pieced center; press seams toward strips.

3. Cut two strips each 2" x 33½" yellow and chocolate prints. Sew a yellow print strip to a chocolate print strip with right sides together along length; press seams toward chocolate print strips. Repeat for two strips.

4. Sew a pieced strip to the top and bottom of the pieced center; press seams toward strips.

5. Cut and piece two strips each dark teal floral 6½" x 42½" and 6½" x 45½". Sew the shorter strips to opposite long sides of the pieced center and the longer strips to the top and bottom; press seams toward strips.

6. Sandwich batting between completed top and prepared backing piece; pin or baste layers together to hold flat.

7. Machine-quilt in the ditch of seams and as desired using clear nylon monofilament in the top of the machine and all-purpose thread in the bobbin.

8. When quilting is complete, remove pins or basting.

9. Bind edges with self-made or purchased binding to finish. ❖

Anniversary Florals

BY MICHELE CRAWFORD

Made with two different floral prints, this Eight-Pointed Star takes on an original look. If you work with contrasting fabrics, your quilt will be as striking as the one pictured here. A perfect present to give as an anniversary present—or to make as a commemoration of your own anniversary.

Anniversary Florals

Project Specifications
Quilt Size: 27" x 27"

Block Size: 9" x 9"

Number of Blocks: 4

Fabric & Batting
- ¼ yard blue floral print
- ¼ yard large floral print
- ⅓ yard each pink and navy prints
- ⅓ yard cream-on-cream print
- Backing 31" x 31"
- Quilter's fleece 31" x 31"
- 3½ yards self-made or purchased binding

Supplies & Tools
- Cream, medium blue and pink all-purpose thread
- Ecru, salmon and delft blue quilting thread
- Basic sewing tools and supplies, rotary cutter, ruler and cutting mat

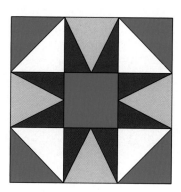

The Eight-Pointed Star
9" x 9" Block

Instructions
1. Prepare templates using pattern pieces given; cut as directed on each piece.

2. To piece one The Eight-Pointed Star block, sew A and AR to B as shown in Figure 1; repeat for 16 A-B units and set aside.

Figure 1
Sew A and AR to B.

Anniversary Florals

1/2" x 18 1/2"

3/4" x 19 1/2"

3/4" x 21"

Anniversary Florals
Placement Diagram
27" x 27"

3. Cut four squares blue floral print 3½" x 3½" for C and 10 squares 3⅞" x 3⅞" for D. Cut each D square in half on one diagonal to make D triangles.

4. Cut 10 squares cream-on-cream print 3⅞" x 3⅞" for D; cut each square in half on one diagonal to make D triangles.

5. Sew a cream-on-cream print D to a blue floral print D as shown in Figure 2; repeat for 20 D units. Set aside four D units for borders.

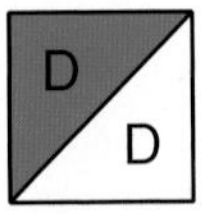

Figure 2
Sew a cream-on-cream print
D to a blue floral print D.

6. Join two D units with an A-B unit to make a row as shown in Figure 3; repeat for two rows.

Figure 3
Join 2 D units with an A-B
unit to make a row.

7. Join two A-B units with a C square to make a row as shown in Figure 4. Join this row with the A-B-D rows to complete one block as shown in Figure 5; repeat for four blocks.

Figure 4
Join 2 A-B units with a C
square to make a row.

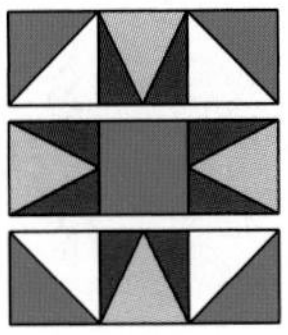

Figure 5
Join rows to
complete 1 block.

8. Cut four 1" x 9½" strips cream-on-cream print for sashing strips. Join two blocks with a sashing strip to make a block row as shown in Figure 6; repeat for two block rows. Press seams toward blocks.

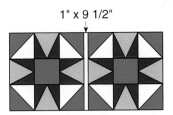

1" x 9 1/2"

Figure 6
Join 2 blocks with a sashing
strip to make a block row.

9. Cut five sashing squares blue floral print 1" x 1". Join two sashing strips with one square to make a sashing row.

Anniversary Florals

10. Join the block rows with the sashing row as shown in Figure 7; press seams toward strips.

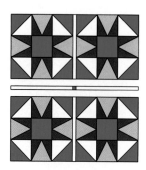

Figure 7
Join the block rows
with the sashing row.

11. Cut four strips 1" x 19" cream-on-cream print. Sew a strip to two opposite sides of the pieced center; press seams toward strips. Sew a sashing square to each end of the remaining two strips; sew these strips to the remaining sides of the pieced center. Press seams toward strips.

12. Cut two strips each pink print 1¼" x 20" and 1¼" x 21½". Sew the shorter strips to the top and bottom and longer strips to remaining sides of the pieced center; press seams toward strips.

13. Cut one strip navy print and two strips large floral print 3½" by fabric width; subcut strips into 3½" square segments for C. You will need 12 navy print and 16 large floral print C squares.

14. Join four large floral print C squares with three navy print C squares to make a strip; repeat for four strips. Sew a strip to two opposites side of the pieced center; press seams toward strips.

15. Sew a D unit to each end of the remaining two strips as shown in Figure 8; sew these strips to the remaining sides of the pieced center referring to the Placement Diagram for positioning.

Figure 8
Sew a D unit to each end of a C strip.

16. Sandwich quilter's fleece between completed top and prepared backing; pin or baste layers together to hold flat.

17. Machine-quilt in the seam around each block C square using delft blue quilting thread, on each side of the sashing strip using ecru quilting thread and in the ditch of the pink print border strips using salmon quilting thread.

18. Hand-quilt down the center of each sashing strip and ¼" from seam on all cream-on-cream print D

triangles using delft blue quilting thread and ¼"
from each seam on the pink border strips using ecru
quilting thread. Use salmon quilting thread to hand-
quilt ¼" in on both sides of navy print C squares in
the borders and to quilt the heart shape given in the
block center squares.

19. When quilting is complete, trim edges even;
remove pins or basting. Bind edges with self-made
or purchased binding to finish. ❖

Heart Quilting Design

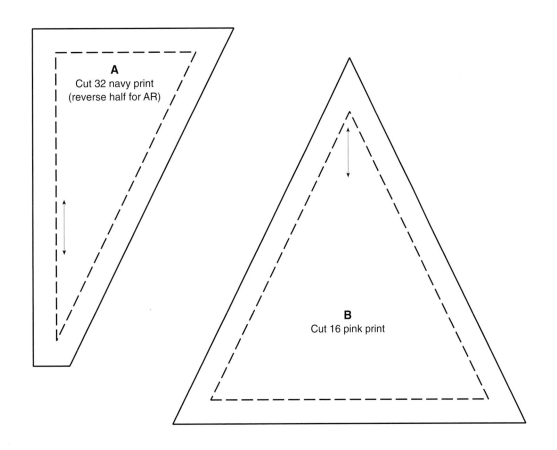

A
Cut 32 navy print
(reverse half for AR)

B
Cut 16 pink print

Windmill Steps

BY JUDITH SANDSTROM

A strip-pieced section joins the eight triangles that make up the traditional Windmill block.   The result is a new block design that creates a fascinating new little quilt. Using the quick strip-piecing methods, this pretty quilt can be finished in record time.

Windmill Steps

Project Specifications
Wall Quilt Size: 25" x 32"
Block Size: 7" x 7"
Number of Blocks: 12

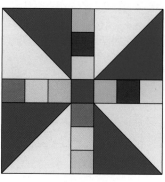

Windmill Steps
7" x 7" Block

Fabric & Batting
- ⅛ yard each of six yellow/blue prints
- ⅜ yard yellow/blue paisley
- ⅜ yard each yellow and blue prints
- Backing 29" x 36"
- Thin cotton batting 29" x 36"
- 3½ yards self-made or purchased binding

Supplies & Tools
- All-purpose thread to match fabrics
- Quilting thread
- Basic sewing tools and supplies and water-soluble pen

Instructions
1. Prewash and iron all fabrics.

2. Cut three strips each 3⅞" by fabric width from yellow and blue prints. Subcut strips into 3⅞" squares. You will need 24 squares of each color. Cut each square in half on one diagonal to make 48 triangles of each color.

3. From the remainder of blue print, cut 12 squares 1½" x 1½".

Windmill Steps

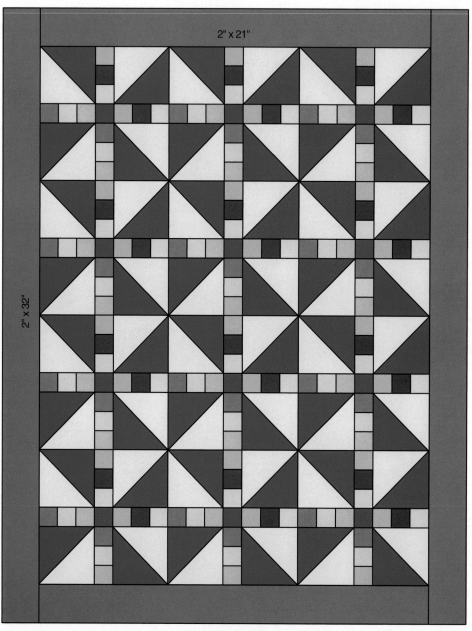

Windmill Steps
Placement Diagram
25" x 32"

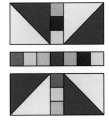

Figure 5
Join 1 of each pieced
unit to complete 1 block.

4. From each yellow/blue print, cut one 1½" by fabric width strip. Assign a number to each strip; stitch strips 1, 2 and 3 together along length as shown in Figure 1. Press seams open. Stitch strips 4, 5 and 6 as before, again referring to Figure 1; press seams open.

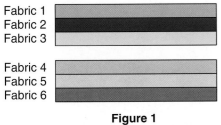

Figure 1
Stitch fabrics 1, 2 and 3 to make a
set; repeat with fabrics 4, 5 and 6.

5. Cut each strip set into 1½" units; you will need 24 of each unit.

6. Stitch each blue print triangle to a yellow print triangle to make a square; press seams open. You will need 48 triangle/squares.

7. Sew a 1-2-3 unit between two triangle/squares as shown in Figure 2; press. Repeat for 12 units. Sew a 4-5-6 unit between two triangle/squares as shown in Figure 3; press. Repeat for 12 units.

Figure 2
Sew a 1-2-3 unit between
2 triangle/squares.

Figure 3
Sew a 4-5-6 unit between
2 triangle/squares.

8. Join a 1-2-3 unit with a blue print 1½" x 1½" square with a 4-5-6 unit as shown in Figure 4; press. Repeat for 12 units.

Figure 4
Sew a 1 1/2" x 1 1/2" blue
print square between a 1-2-3
and a 4-5-6 unit as shown.

9. Join one of each pieced unit as shown in Figure 5 to complete one block; repeat for 12 blocks; press.

10. Arrange blocks in four rows of three blocks each referring to the Placement Diagram for positioning of blocks. Join blocks in rows; join rows to complete pieced center.

11. Cut two strips each yellow/blue paisley 2½" x 21½" and 2½" x 32½". Sew a short strip to the top and bottom and the longer strips to opposite sides of the pieced center; press seams toward strips.

12. Sandwich thin cotton batting between completed top and prepared backing piece; pin or baste layers together.

13. Quilt as desired by hand or machine. When quilting is complete, trim edges even; remove pins or basting.

14. Bind edges with self-made or purchased binding to finish. ❖

Paisley Lilies

BY LUCY A. FAZELY

The lilies come from the traditional Lily block; the paisley from a paisley print fabric. Combined you can construct these beautiful paisley lilies. By using a pale print for the sashing and borders, the paisley lilies will seem to float on the background in this pretty little wall quilt.

Paisley Lily
14" x 14" Block

Paisley Lilies

Project Specifications

Quilt Size: 42" x 42"
Block Size: 14" x 14"
Number of Blocks: 4

Fabric & Batting

- ⅛ yard violet paisley print
- 1 yard rose paisley print
- 1⅛ yards white-on-green print
- 1⅜ yards plum print
- Backing 46" x 46"
- Batting 46" x 46"

Supplies & Tools

- Neutral color all-purpose thread
- Clear nylon monofilament
- Basic sewing tools and supplies

Instructions

1. Prepare templates A–F using pattern pieces given. Cut as directed on each piece for one block; repeat for four blocks.

2. To piece one block, sew B to opposite sides of A. Sew C to opposite short ends of B; repeat. Sew C-B-C units to opposite sides of the B-A-B unit.

3. Sew a D triangle to each side of the A-B-C unit as shown in Figure 1.

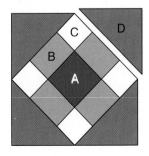

Figure 1
Sew D to the A-B-C unit as shown.

Paisley Lilies

2" x 34"

Paisley Lilies
Placement Diagram
42" x 42"

4. Sew E to two adjacent short sides of F; repeat for eight units. Join two units with C; repeat for four units. Sew an E-F-C unit to opposite sides of the A-B-C-D unit as shown in Figure 2.

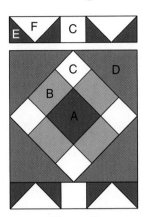

Figure 2
Sew an E-F-C unit to opposite
sides of the A-B-C-D unit.

5. Sew C to each end of the remaining two E-F-C units and sew to the remaining sides of the pieced unit as shown in Figure 3 to complete one block. Repeat for four blocks.

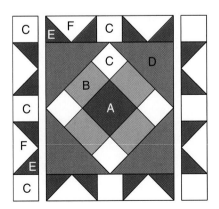

Figure 3
Join pieced units as shown.

6. Cut two strips 2½" x 14½" and three strips 2½" x 30½" white-on-green print.

7. Join two blocks with a 2½" x 14½" strip white-on-green print to make a block row as shown in Figure 4; press seams toward strip. Repeat for second block row.

Figure 4
Join 2 blocks with a 2 1/2" x 14 1/2" strip
white-on-green print to make a block row.

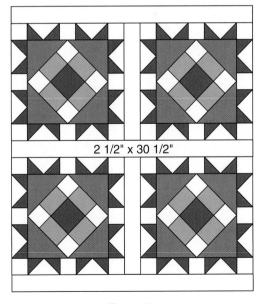

Figure 5
Join the block rows with the
2 1/2" x 30 1/2" strips as shown.

Paisley Lilies

8. Join the block rows with the 2½" x 30½" white-on-green print strips, beginning and ending with a strip referring to Figure 5; press seams toward strips.

9. Cut two strips white-on-green print 2½" x 34½"; sew to sides of the pieced center. Press seams toward strips.

10. Prepare templates G–I for borders using pattern pieces given; cut as directed on each piece.

11. Sew two white-on-green print I pieces to a rose paisley print G piece as shown in Figure 6; repeat for 68 units. Join 17 units as shown in Figure 7 to make a side row; repeat for four rows.

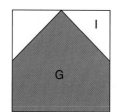

Figure 6
Sew 2 white-on-green
print I pieces to a rose
paisley print G piece.

Figure 7
Join 17 units as shown to make a side row.

12. Sew an I-G row to opposite sides of the pieced center; press seams away from pieced rows.

13. Sew a white-with-green print I to rose paisley print H; repeat for four units. Sew an I-H unit to each end of a pieced I-G row as shown in Figure 8; repeat. Sew these strips to the remaining sides of the pieced center.

Figure 8
Sew an I-H unit to each end of a pieced I-G row.

14. Sew two rose paisley print I pieces to a plum print G; repeat for 76 units. Join 19 units to make a side row; repeat for four rows.

15. Sew an I-G row to opposite sides of the pieced center; press seams away from pieced rows.

16. Sew a rose paisley print I to a plum print H; repeat for four units. Sew an I-H unit to each end of a pieced I-G row as shown in Figure 9; repeat. Sew

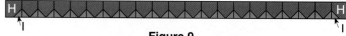

Figure 9
Sew an I-H unit to each end of a pieced I-G row.

these strips to the remaining sides of the pieced center to complete pieced top.

17. Sandwich batting between completed top and prepared backing piece; pin or baste layers together to hold.

18. Quilt as desired by hand or machine. *Note: The quilt shown was machine-quilted in a meandering pattern in the background using clear nylon mono-* *filament in the top of the machine and white all-purpose thread in the bobbin.*

19. When quilting is complete, trim edges even and remove pins or basting. Bind edges with self-made or purchased binding to finish. *Note: The quilt shown was bound with self-made plum print binding to match the fabric in the quilt.* ❖

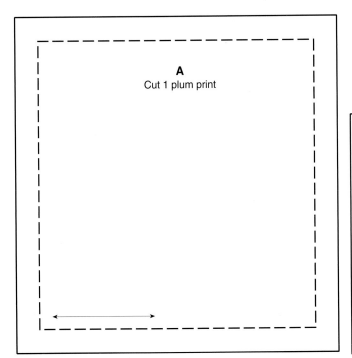

A
Cut 1 plum print

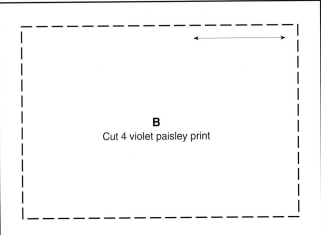

B
Cut 4 violet paisley print

Paisley Lilies

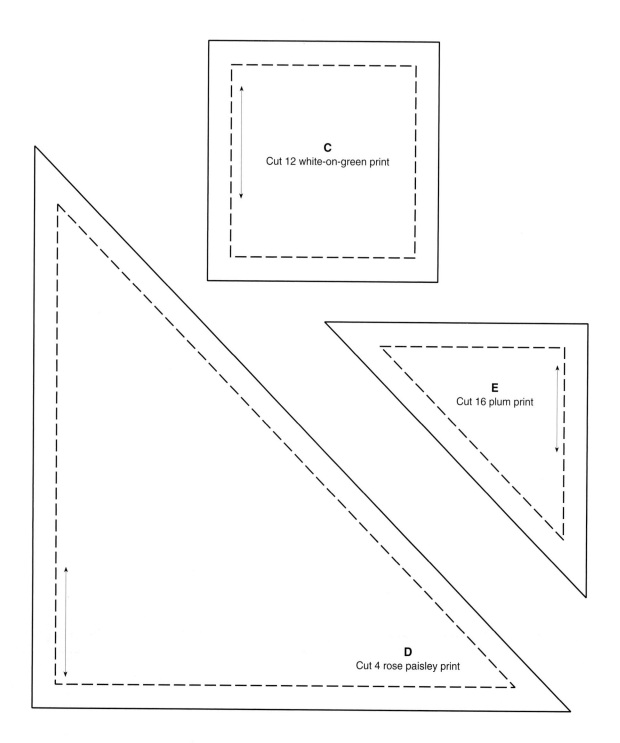

C
Cut 12 white-on-green print

E
Cut 16 plum print

D
Cut 4 rose paisley print

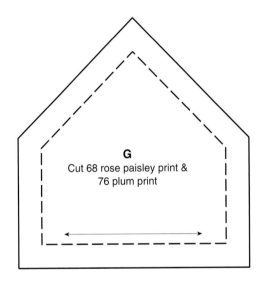

G
Cut 68 rose paisley print &
76 plum print

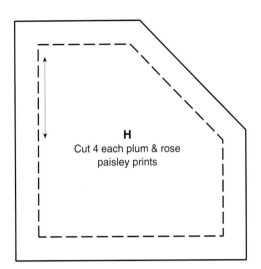

H
Cut 4 each plum & rose
paisley prints

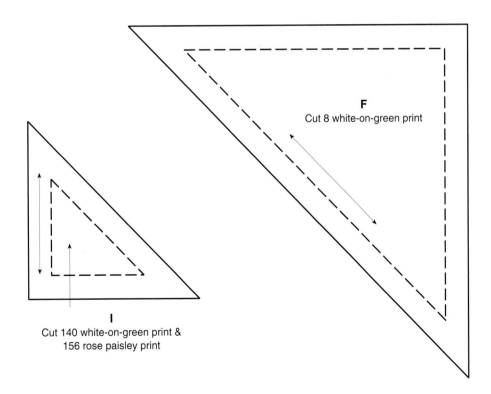

F
Cut 8 white-on-green print

I
Cut 140 white-on-green print &
156 rose paisley print

China Blue Basket

BY CYNTHIA SULLIVAN

Here is a quilt for all those antique blue and white china collectors! This charming tiny quilt would make the perfect foil for a collector's display. If you collect blue fabrics, this is certainly the place to use them—or try making the quilt in a combination of your favorite colors.

China Blue Basket
10" x 10" Block

China Blue Basket

Project Specifications
Quilt Size: 32" x 32"
Block Size: 10" x 10"
Number of Blocks: 1

Fabric & Batting
- ⅛ yard muslin
- ¼ yard medium floral print
- ¼ yard medium blue print
- ¼ yard dark blue print
- ¾ yard mottled blue print
- ¾ yard large floral print
- Backing 36" x 36"
- Batting 36" x 36"
- 4 yards self-made or purchased binding

Supplies & Tools
- Neutral color all-purpose thread

- Basic sewing tools and supplies, rotary cutter, ruler and cutting mat

Instructions
1. Prepare templates using pattern pieces given. Cut as directed on each piece.

2. To piece block, join A triangles to make squares referring to Figure 1.

Make 6

Make 3

Make 2

Make 2

Make 1

Figure 1
Join A triangles to make
squares as shown.

China Blue Basket

4" x 32"   1/2" x 18"

1" x 22"

1 1/2" x 22"

1/2" x 19"

1" x 24"

1 1/2" x 22"

China Blue Basket
Placement Diagram
32" x 32"

COLOR KEY
☐ Muslin
☐ Medium floral print
☐ Medium blue print
☐ Dark blue print
☐ Mottled blue print
☐ Large floral print

3. Arrange A units with A triangles, B, C and D as shown in Figure 2; join in rows. Join rows to complete one block; press.

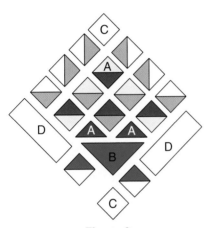

Figure 2
Join pieces to complete 1 block.

4. Cut two strips each mottled blue print $1^7/8$" x $10^1/2$" and $1^7/8$" x $13^1/4$". Sew the shorter strips to two opposite sides and longer strips to remaining sides as shown in Figure 3; press seams toward strips.

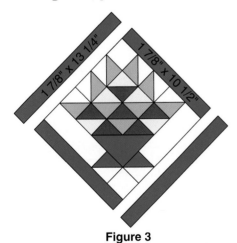

Figure 3
Sew strips to sides
of block as shown.

5. Join E triangles to make units as shown in Figure 4. Join the units as shown in Figure 5 to make pieced corners; repeat for four corners.

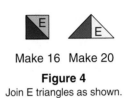

Make 16   Make 20
Figure 4
Join E triangles as shown.

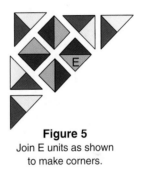

Figure 5
Join E units as shown
to make corners.

6. Cut two strips each dark blue print 1" x $18^1/2$" and 1" x $19^1/2$". Sew the shorter strips to the top and bottom and longer strips to opposite sides; press seams toward strips.

7. Cut four strips medium floral print 2" x $22^1/2$". Sew a strip to each side of the pieced section, mitering corners. Press seams toward strips.

8. Cut two strips each mottled blue print $1^1/2$" x $22^1/2$" and $1^1/2$" x $24^1/2$". Sew the shorter strips to the top and bottom and longer strips to opposite sides; press seams toward strips.

9. Cut four strips 4½" x 32½" large floral print. Fold each strip in half and crease to mark center.

10. Prepare F pieces for appliqué. Using center creases as a guide for placement, hand-appliqué six F pieces on each 4½" x 32½" large floral print strip placing the raw edge of F on the raw edge of the strip as shown in Figure 6. Repeat on each strip.

11. Center and sew an appliquéd strip to each side

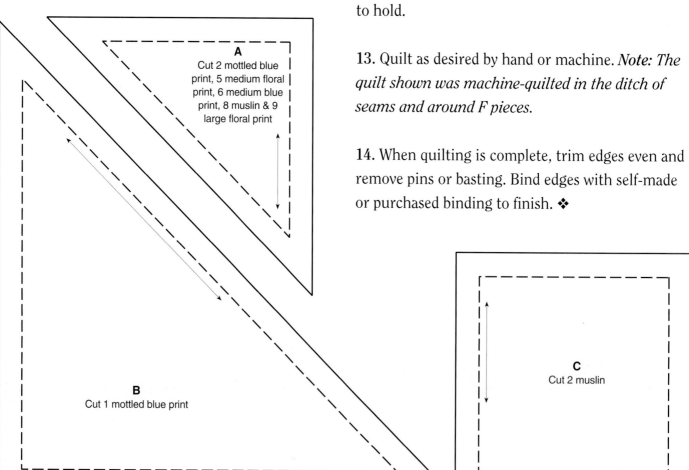

Figure 6
Place 6 F pieces on each 4 1/2" x 32 1/2" strip using center crease as a guide for placement and aligning raw edge of F with raw edge of strip.

of the pieced section, mitering corners. Press seams toward strips.

12. Sandwich batting between completed top and prepared backing piece; pin or baste layers together to hold.

13. Quilt as desired by hand or machine. *Note: The quilt shown was machine-quilted in the ditch of seams and around F pieces.*

14. When quilting is complete, trim edges even and remove pins or basting. Bind edges with self-made or purchased binding to finish. ❖

A
Cut 2 mottled blue print, 5 medium floral print, 6 medium blue print, 8 muslin & 9 large floral print

B
Cut 1 mottled blue print

C
Cut 2 muslin

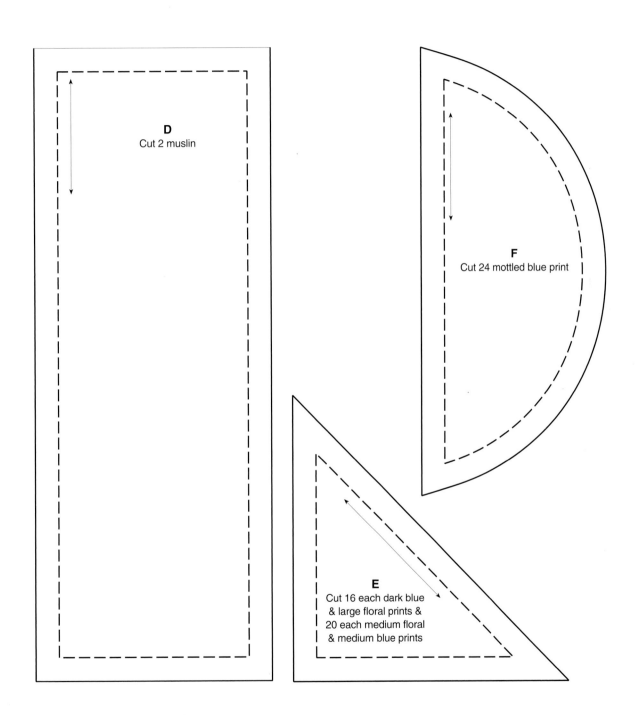

D
Cut 2 muslin

F
Cut 24 mottled blue print

E
Cut 16 each dark blue
& large floral prints &
20 each medium floral
& medium blue prints

Impressions Wall Quilt

BY MICHELE CRAWFORD

Here is a quilt that will certainly leave a lasting impression on all who see it. Piecing the quilt will take very little time, especially if you follow the quick and easy instructions. After the quilt has been pieced, there is room for both machine and hand quilting that will give it an heirloom quality. As a final touch, sew four buttons on the red squares of the plaid border corners.

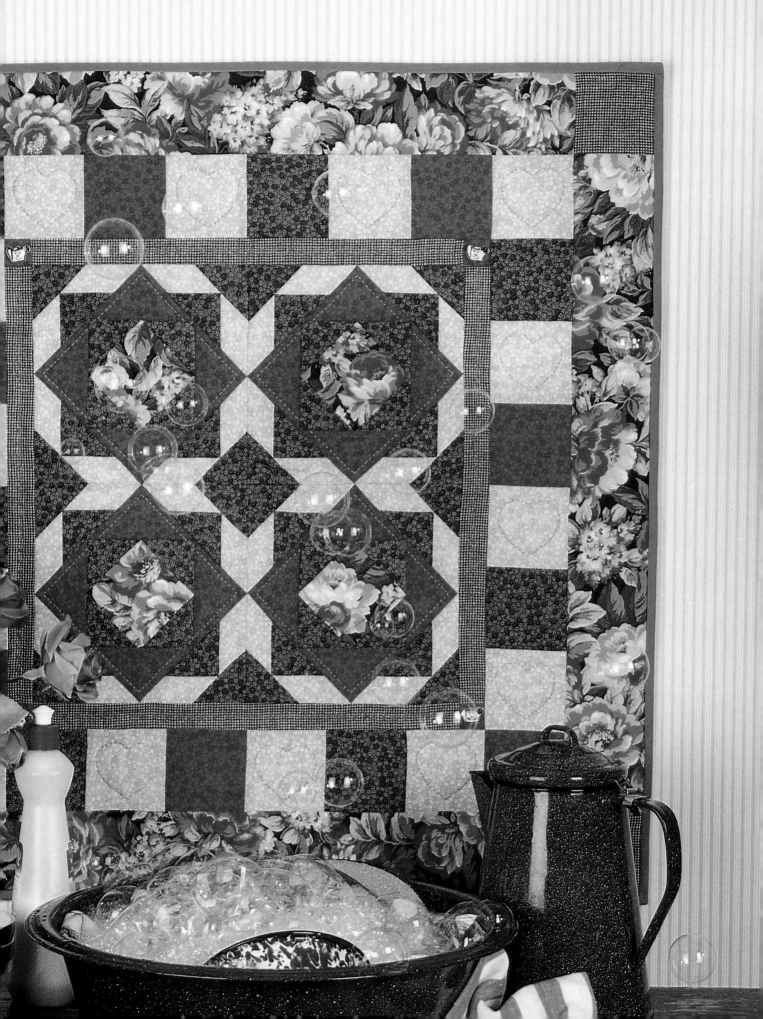

Impressions Wall Quilt

3" x 3"

1" x 1"

3" x 24"

3" x 3"

Impressions Wall Quilt
Placement Diagram
30" x 30"

Impressions Wall Quilt

Impressions
8" x 8" Block

Project Specifications

Quilt Size: 30" x 30"

Block Size: 8" x 8"

Number of Blocks: 4

Fabric & Batting

- $\frac{1}{8}$ yard small green plaid
- $\frac{1}{6}$ yard dark blue small floral print
- $\frac{1}{4}$ yard each taupe and red small floral prints
- $1\frac{1}{2}$ yards navy large floral print
- Cotton batting 34" x 34"
- 2 packages stone blue wide bias tape

Supplies & Tools

- 1 spool each rose, blue and cream all-purpose thread
- 1 spool each light tan, cornflower blue and dark mauve quilting thread
- 4 ceramic watering can buttons
- $\frac{1}{4}$" masking tape
- Basic sewing supplies and tools, rotary cutter, ruler and cutting mat

Instructions

Note: Use a $\frac{1}{4}$" seam allowance. Sew pieces with right sides together and raw edges even with matching thread. Press seam allowance toward darkest fabric.

1. Prepare template for A. Cut as directed. Cut the following to piece four blocks: red—eight $3\frac{3}{4}$" x $3\frac{3}{4}$" squares, cut each square on the diagonal to make 16 R triangles; blue—24 squares $2\frac{7}{8}$" x $2\frac{7}{8}$", cut each square in half on the diagonal to make 48 B triangles; and large floral—four $3\frac{3}{8}$" x $3\frac{3}{8}$" squares for F.

2. Referring to Figure 1, sew pieces A and AR to adjacent short sides of B. Sew a B piece to the B point side of this unit; repeat for four units. Sew B to each side of F; sew R to each side of the B-F unit.

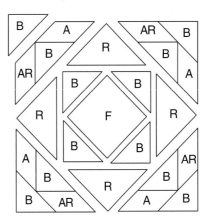

Figure 1
Join pieces in units; join
units to complete 1 block.

Impressions Wall Quilt

Sew an A-B unit to each side of the B-F-R center to complete one block. Repeat for four blocks; press.

3. Cut four strips small green plaid 1½" x 16½". Cut four squares red 1½" x 1½". Sew a strip to opposite sides of the pieced center. Sew a square to each end of the remaining two strips; sew a strip to each of the remaining two sides. Press.

4. Cut seven squares each dark blue and red and 14 squares taupe 3½" x 3½". Referring to Figure 2, arrange the squares around the center. Join in strips; sew strips to sides and top and bottom. Press.

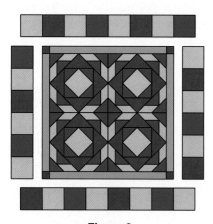

Figure 2
Arrange squares around
pieced center for borders.

5. Cut four strips large floral print 3½" x 24½" and four squares green plaid 3½" x 3½". Sew a strip

to opposite sides; sew a square to each end to the remaining two strips. Sew to top and bottom; press.

6. Cut a 32" x 32" square large floral print for backing. Center the wrong side of the quilt on the batting; pin or baste layers together.

7. Machine-quilt in the ditch of the seams around the blue square in each block with cornflower blue thread. Repeat in the rose squares with dark mauve thread.

8. Using dark mauve thread and a decorative machine flower stitch, stitch down the center of each green plaid strip.

9. Hand-quilt a heart in the center of each taupe square on pieced border using design given and cornflower blue thread. Repeat in the center of each block and in outside border squares with dark mauve thread.

10. Using masking tape as a guide, hand-quilt ¼" inside each red print triangle in the blocks using light tan thread.

11. Sew a watering can button in each small red

square in green plaid border corners.

12. When quilting is complete, remove pins or basting. Trim excess batting and backing even with quilt top.

13. Bind edges with wide bias tape, mitering corners and overlapping ends to finish. ❖

Heart Quilting Design

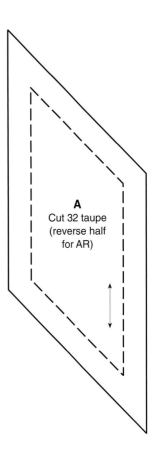

A
Cut 32 taupe
(reverse half
for AR)

Art Nouveau Garden

BY ALEXANDRIA CAPADALIS DUPRE

Cotton sateen fabrics give this wall quilt an extra sparkle. Combine the sateen cottons with fat quarters from your fabric collection, and you'll create an arty quilt fit to hang on the wall of a museum. The garden motif print used in the sample quilt is a one-way print that must be cut on the lengthwise grain for the side pieces and the crosswise grain for the top and bottom pieces. The fabric requirements listed reflect this. If your choice of fabric is not a one-way print, you will need much less fabric.

Art Nouveau Garden

4" x 42"

3" x 36"

Art Nouveau Garden
Placement Diagram
42" x 44"

Art Nouveau Garden

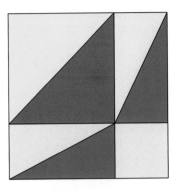

Art Nouveau
6" x 6" Block

Project Specifications

Quilt Size: 42" x 44"

Block Size: 6" x 6"

Number of Blocks: 36

Fabric & Batting

- 12–14 fat quarters light-to-medium prints
- ³/₈ yard each pink and rose solid cotton sateens
- ½ yard green solid cotton sateens
- 1³/₈ yards garden motif
- Backing 46" x 48"
- Batting 46" x 48"
- 5¼ yards self-made or purchased binding

Supplies & Tools

- Neutral color all-purpose thread
- White machine-quilting thread
- Basic sewing tools and supplies, rotary cutter, ruler and cutting mat

Instructions

1. Cut five strips green sateen 2³/₄" by fabric width; subcut into 5¹/₈" segments. Cut each segment in half on the diagonal to make A and AR triangles as shown in Figure 1; you will need 36 A and 36 AR solid triangles.

2. Cut 72 light-to-medium print 2³/₄" x 5¹/₈" rectangles in half on the diagonal to make A and AR triangles as shown in Figure 1. You will need 36 A and 36 AR print triangles.

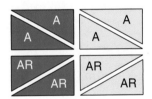

Figure 1
Cut each rectangle in half
on the diagonal to make
A and AR triangles.

3. Sew a solid A to a print A and a solid AR to a print AR as shown in Figure 2; repeat for 36 each A and AR units.

4. Cut 36 squares light-to-medium prints 2½" x 2½" for B.

Art Nouveau Garden

Figure 2
Sew a solid A to a print A and
a solid AR to a print AR.

5. Cut two strips each 4⅞" by fabric width pink and rose solid sateens; subcut each strip into 4⅞" square segments. Cut each square in half on one diagonal to make solid C triangles. You will need 36 solid C triangles.

6. Cut 18 squares light-to-medium prints 4⅞" x 4⅞"; cut each square in half on one diagonal to make print C triangles.

7. Sew a print C to a solid C along the diagonal as shown in Figure 3; repeat for 36 units.

Figure 3
Sew a print C to a solid
C along the diagonal.

8. Sew an A unit to one solid side of a C unit referring to Figure 4. Sew B to one end of an AR unit and sew to the remaining solid side of the pieced unit to complete one block, again referring to Figure 4; repeat for 36 blocks.

Figure 4
Join units as shown
to complete 1 block.

9. Arrange the blocks in six rows of six blocks each referring to the Placement Diagram for positioning of blocks in each row.

10. Join the blocks in rows; press seams in one direction. Join rows to complete the pieced center; press seams in one direction.

11. Cut two strips garden motif 4½" x 42½" across width of fabric; cut two strips 3½" x 36½" along length of fabric. Sew the shorter strips to opposite sides and longer strips to the top and bottom of the pieced center; press seams toward strips. *Note: The garden motif used in the sample is a one-way print that must be cut on the lengthwise grain for the*

side pieces and the crosswise grain for the top and bottom pieces. This fact is reflected in the fabric amounts listed as more fabric is needed for this type of print.

12. Sandwich batting between completed top and prepared backing piece; pin or baste layers together to hold flat.

13. Quilt as desired by hand or machine. *Note: The quilt shown was machine-quilted in the ditch of seams using white machine-quilting thread.*

14. When quilting is complete, trim edges even; remove pins or basting.

15. Bind edges with self-made or purchased binding to finish. ❖

Princess Stars

BY LUCY A. FAZELY

The 16 Princess stars are created quickly using the quick-piecing methods listed in the instructions and are joined with quick-to-make sashing strips. You can make the entire wall hanging in a weekend, and then stand back and receive compliments for years. While the stars may be princesses, you'll feel like a queen after you have completed this fun project.

Princess Stars

2 1/4" x 50 3/4"

Princess Stars
Placement Diagram
50 3/4" x 50 3/4"

Princess Stars

Project Specifications

Quilt Size: 50¾" x 50¾"

Block Size: 10" x 10"

Number of Blocks: 16

Fabric & Batting

- ⅛ yard each of 11 coordinating prints
- ⅛ yard print for sashing squares
- ¼ yard each 3 coordinating floral prints
- 1½ yards white print for background
- 2 yards border stripe
- Backing 55" x 55"
- Batting 55" x 55"
- 6¼ yards self-made or purchased binding

Supplies & Tools

- Matching all-purpose thread
- Basic sewing tools and supplies, rotary cutter, ruler and cutting mat

Instructions

1. Cut 14 strips background fabric 3" by fabric width. Cut 64 squares 3" x 3" and 64 rectangles 3" x 5½" from the strips.

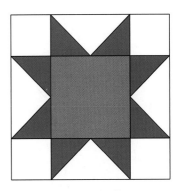

Princess Star
10" x 10" Block

2. Cut 16 squares 5½" x 5½" from the coordinating floral prints.

3. For each block, cut eight 3" x 3" squares coordinating print.

4. Draw one diagonal line on each 3" x 3" coordinating print square. Place one of these squares right sides together on one end of a 3" x 5½" rectangle as shown in Figure 1.

Figure 1
Place a square on the corner of the rectangle.

Princess Stars

5. Sew along the marked stitching line on the square; trim seam to 1/4" as shown in Figure 2. Press seam toward the coordinating print. Repeat on the opposite end of the background rectangle to make a Flying Geese unit as shown in Figure 3. Repeat for four units.

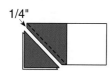

Figure 2
Sew along marked stitching
line; trim seam to 1/4"

Figure 3
Repeat on opposite end of
background rectangle to make a
Flying Geese unit.

6. Sew a 3" x 3" background square to each end of two Flying Geese units.

7. Arrange pieced units with a 5½" x 5½" coordinating floral print square; join as shown in Figure 4 to make one block. Press and repeat for 16 blocks.

Figure 4
Arrange pieced units as
shown to make 1 block.

8. Select a section from the border print to use for sashing strips. Cut 40 identical sashing strips 1¾" x 10½".

9. Cut 25 squares from sashing square fabric 1¾" x 1¾".

10. Join four blocks with five sashing strips to make a row as shown in Figure 5; press. Repeat for four rows.

1 3/4" x 10 1/2"

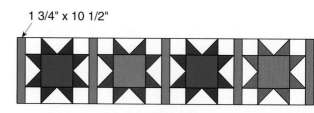

Figure 5
Join 4 blocks with 5 sashing strips.

11. Join five sashing squares with four sashing strips to make a row as shown in Figure 6; press. Repeat for five rows.

1 3/4" x 1 3/4"   1 3/4" x 10 1/2"

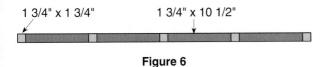

Figure 6
Join 5 sashing squares with 4 sashing strips.

12. Join the block rows with the sashing rows, beginning and ending with a sashing row; press.

13. Cut four strips 2¾" x 51¼" from border stripe. Fold each strip to find center; crease and pin.

14. Pin a strip to each side of the pieced center, matching center of strip on center of quilt. Pin and stitch in place, mitering corners. Trim excess from miter; press seams toward strips.

15. Sandwich batting between prepared backing and completed quilt top. Pin or baste layers together to hold flat for quilting.

16. Quilt as desired by hand or machine.

17. When quilting is complete, trim edges even. Bind with self-made or purchased binding to finish. ❖

Fiery Baskets

BY CHRISTINE CARLSON

Miniature bright pink baskets float on a white background in this tiny square quilt. The baskets in the center are easy to create and quick to finish, leaving room and time to hand-quilt the quilting designs in the triangles at the sides and in the borders. If hand quilting is your favorite, this would be a fun quilt to make.

Fiery Baskets

Fiery Baskets
Placement Diagram
14 1/8" x 14 1/8"
(includes binding)

Fiery Baskets

Project Specifications

Quilt Size: 14⅛" x 14⅛" (includes binding)

Block Size: 3¾" x 3¾"

Number of Blocks: 4

Fabric & Batting

- 1 fat quarter bright print
- ¼ yard pink print
- ¼ yard white solid
- Backing 17" x 17"
- Batting 17" x 17"
- 1¾ yards self-made or purchased narrow white binding

Supplies & Tools

- Neutral color all-purpose thread
- White quilting thread
- Basic sewing tools and supplies and water-erasable marker or pen

Instructions

1. Prepare templates using pattern pieces given; cut as directed on each piece.

2. To piece one block, sew a white solid A to a bright print A as shown in Figure 1; repeat for six A units.

3. Join three A units as shown in Figure 2; repeat.

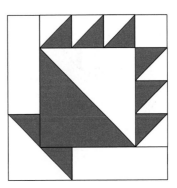

Fiery Basket
3 3/4" x 3 3/4" Block

Figure 1
Sew a white solid A
to a bright print A.

Make 1

Make 1

Figure 2
Join 3 A units.

4. Sew a white solid B to a bright print B along the diagonals.

5. Sew an A unit to one white solid side of the B unit. Sew C to the bright print A end of the remaining A unit and sew to the A-B unit as shown in Figure 3.

6. Sew a bright print A to one end of D as shown in Figure 4; repeat for two A-D units.

Figure 3
Sew C to the bright print A
end of the remaining A unit
and sew to the A-B unit.

Make 1

Make 1

Figure 4
Sew a bright print
A to 1 end of D.

7. Sew an A-D unit to the B sides of the A-B-C unit as shown in Figure 5. Add E to the corner to complete one block as shown in Figure 6; repeat for four blocks.

Fiery Baskets

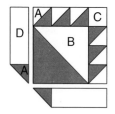

Figure 5
Sew an A-D unit to the B
sides of the A-B-C unit.

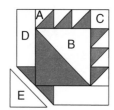

Figure 6
Add E to
complete 1 block.

8. Join the four blocks as shown in Figure 7; press seams in one direction.

Figure 7
Join the 4 blocks
as shown.

Figure 8
Sew an F triangle to
each side of the pieced
section as shown.

9. Sew an F triangle to each side of the pieced section as shown in Figure 8; press seams toward F.

10. Cut four strips pink print 2" x 11⅛"; sew a strip to two opposite sides of the pieced center. Press seams toward strips.

11. Sew a white solid G to a bright print G as shown in Figure 9; repeat for eight units. Join two units as shown in Figure 10 to make a G corner unit; repeat for four units.

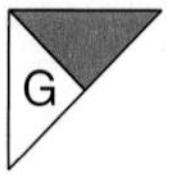

Figure 9
Sew a white solid G
to a bright print G.

Figure 10
Join 2 units
as shown.

12. Sew a G unit to each end of the remaining 2" x 11⅛" bright print strips as shown in Figure 11; repeat for two strip units. Sew a strip to each remaining side of the pieced center to complete the top; press seams toward strips.

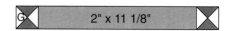

Figure 11
Sew a G unit to each end of
the remaining 2" x 11 1/8"
bright print strips.

13. Mark the quilting designs given in the F triangles and borders using a water-erasable marker or pen.

14. Sandwich batting between the completed top and prepared backing; pin or baste layers together to hold flat.

15. Hand-quilt on marked lines using white quilting thread.

16. When quilting is complete, remove pins or basting; trim edges even.

17. Bind with self-made or purchased binding to finish. *Note: The quilt shown has pink print binding on each corner unit and white solid binding along remaining edges.* ❖

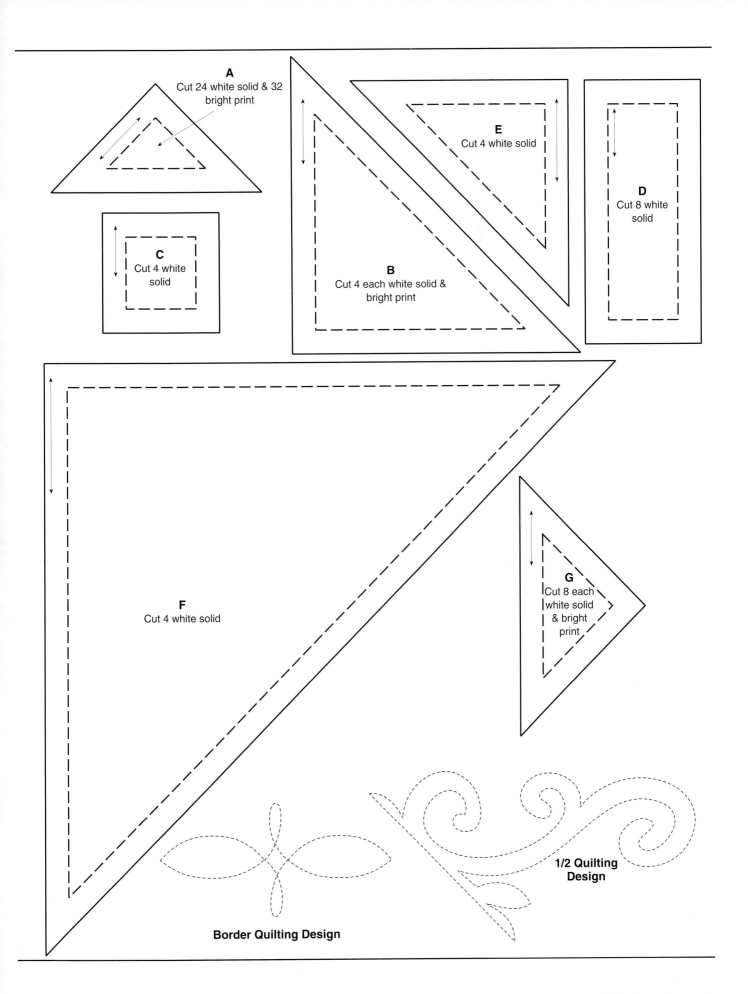

A
Cut 24 white solid & 32 bright print

C
Cut 4 white solid

B
Cut 4 each white solid & bright print

E
Cut 4 white solid

D
Cut 8 white solid

F
Cut 4 white solid

G
Cut 8 each white solid & bright print

Border Quilting Design

1/2 Quilting Design

Splendor

BY MICHELE CRAWFORD

Sometimes the simplest quilts are the most splendid, and Splendor is the perfect name for this simple triangle/square quilt. Gold and green prints are combined in easy-to-sew blocks that when joined make a most lovely wall quilt. This quilt is a great project for a beginner and would look terrific in any home!

Splendor

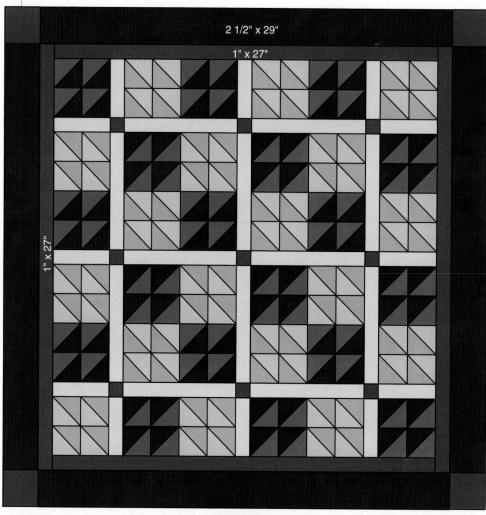

Splendor
Placement Diagram
34" x 34"

Splendor

Project Specifications

Quilt Size: 34" x 34"

Block Size: 4" x 4"

Number of Blocks: 36

Fabric & Batting

- ¼ yard pink print
- ⅓ yard each dark gold, light gold, light green and burgundy prints
- ⅔ yard dark green print
- Backing 38" x 38"
- Quilter's fleece 38" x 38"
- 4¼ yards self-made or purchased binding

Supplies & Tools

- Light pink, barberry red, London tan and forest green all-purpose thread
- Clear nylon monofilament
- Basic sewing tools and supplies, rotary cutter, ruler and cutting mat

Instructions

1. Cut three strips each light and dark green prints 2⅞" by fabric width; subcut each strip into 2⅞" square segments. Cut each segment in half on one diagonal to make 72 A triangles for Block A. Repeat with light and dark gold prints for Block B.

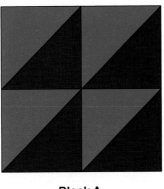

Block A
4" x 4"

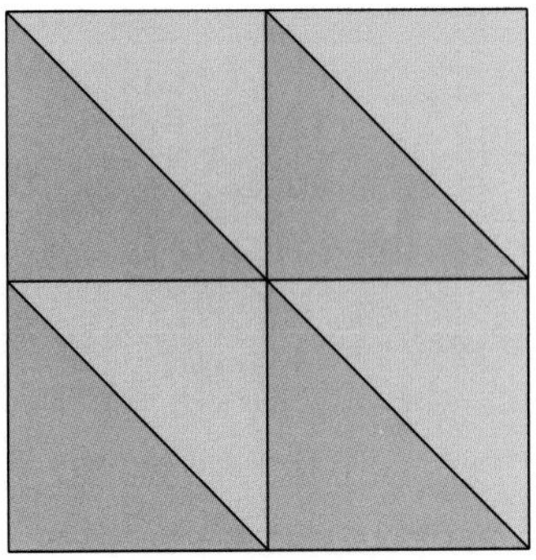

Block B
4" x 4"

2. Join a light and dark green print A on the diagonal to make a triangle/square unit as shown in Figure 1; repeat for all A triangles. Repeat with light and dark gold print B triangles.

3. Join four A units to complete Block A as shown in Figure 2; repeat for 18 blocks. Repeat with four B units to complete Block B as shown in Figure 3; repeat for 18 blocks.

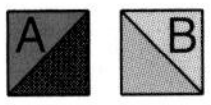

Figure 1
Join 2 A triangles as shown; repeat with 2 B triangles.

Figure 2
Join 4 A units to complete Block A.

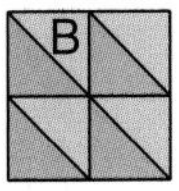

Figure 3
Join 4 B units to complete Block B.

4. Join two each A and B blocks as shown in Figure 4; repeat for four AA/BB block units. Join one each A and B blocks as shown in Figure 5; repeat for eight A/B block units.

Splendor

Figure 4
Join 2 each A
and B blocks.

Make 4

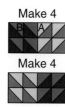

Make 4

Figure 5
Join 1 each A
and B blocks.

1 1/2" x 8 1/2"

A/B   AA/BB   AA/BB   A/B

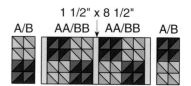

Figure 7
Join 2 AA/BB block units
with 2 A/B block units
and 3 long sashing
strips to make a row.

5. Cut four strips pink print 1½" by fabric width; subcut into 12 each 8½" long sashing strips and 4½" short sashing strips.

6. Cut nine 1½" x 1½" burgundy print sashing squares.

7. Join one each A and B blocks with two A/B block units and three short sashing strips to make a row as shown in Figure 6; repeat for two rows. Press seams toward short sashing strips.

1 1/2" x 4 1/2"

A   A/B   A/B   B

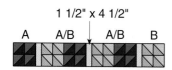

Figure 6
Join 1 each A and B blocks with
2 A/B block units and 3 short
sashing strips to make a row.

8. Join two AA/BB block units with two A/B block units and three long sashing strips to make a row as shown in Figure 7; repeat for two rows.

9. Join two short and two long sashing strips with three sashing squares to make a sashing row as shown in Figure 8; repeat for three sashing rows.

1 1/2" x 4 12"   1 1/2" x 8 1/2"   1 1/2" x 1 1/2"

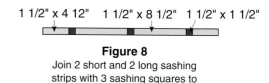

Figure 8
Join 2 short and 2 long sashing
strips with 3 sashing squares to
make a sashing row.

10. Join the block rows with the sashing rows as shown in Figure 9 to complete the pieced center; press seams toward sashing rows.

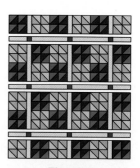

Figure 9
Join the block rows with the
sashing rows as shown to
complete the pieced center.

11. Cut two strips each 1½" x 27½" and 1½" x 29½" burgundy print. Sew the shorter strips to the top and bottom and longer strips to opposite sides; press seams toward strips.

12. Cut four strips 3" x 29½" dark green print and four 3" x 3" squares burgundy print.

13. Sew a dark green print strip to two opposite sides of the pieced center; press seams toward strips. Sew a burgundy print square to each end of the remaining two strips and sew these to the remaining sides of the pieced center; press seams toward strips.

14. Sandwich batting between completed top and prepared backing; pin or baste to hold.

15. Quilt as desired by hand or machine. *Note: The quilt shown was machine-quilted in a curved line through the pink print sashing strips using barberry red all-purpose thread and in the ditch of seams using clear nylon monofilament in the top of the machine and all-purpose thread in the bobbin.*

16. When quilting is complete, remove pins or basting. Trim edges even with quilted top. Bind edges with self-made or purchased binding to finish. ❖

Fall Peaks

BY JUDITH SANDSTROM

As leaves change color in the fall, nature shows us some beautiful colors, and this quilt certainly mirrors the colors of the fall foliage. The peaks are easy to complete with these simple instructions. When all of the triangles are joined, the quilt is reminiscent of mountain peaks covered with beautiful fall trees.

Fall Peaks

Project Specifications
Quilt Size: 32" x 41"

Fabric & Batting
- ⅛ yard each 2 green, 2 gold and 2 orange prints
- ⅜ yard border print
- 1 yard black solid
- Backing 36" x 45"
- Batting 36" x 45"
- 4½ yards self-made or purchased binding

Supplies & Tools
- Neutral color all-purpose thread
- Basic sewing tools and supplies, rotary cutter, ruler and cutting mat

Instructions

1. Cut six 7¼" x 7¼" A squares and four 9⅞" x 9⅞" B squares black solid. Cut each square in half on one diagonal to make triangles.

2. Cut three strips black solid 3" by fabric width; subcut strips into 3" square segments for C. Cut each square in half on one diagonal to make C triangles; you will need 60 C triangles.

3. Cut one 3" by fabric width strip from each of the six prints. Cut each strip into ten 3" square segments for C. Cut each square in half on one diagonal to make C triangles; you will need 20 triangles of each fabric.

Fall Peaks

2 1/2" x 32"

2 1/2" x 36"

Fall Peaks
Placement Diagram
32" x 41"

4. Stitch a print C to a black solid C to make a C-C unit; repeat for 10 C-C units from each print.

5. Join C-C units with three C triangles to make a triangle unit as shown in Figure 1. *Note: Be sure to use one triangle of each of the 6 fabrics in each triangle unit.*

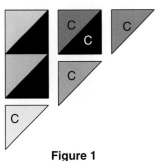

Figure 1
Join C-C units with C as shown.

6. Arrange five pieced C triangle units with A and B triangles as shown in Figure 2; stitch together to make a section. Repeat for four sections; press.

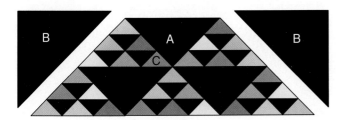

Figure 2
Arrange C units with A and B triangles.

7. Join the four sections to complete pieced center; press seams in one direction.

8. Cut two strips each border print 3" x 32½" and 3" x 36½". Sew the longer strips to opposite sides and shorter strips to top and bottom; press seams toward strips.

9. Sandwich batting between completed top and prepared backing piece; pin or baste layers together to hold.

10. Quilt as desired by hand or machine.

11. When quilting is complete, remove pins or basting, trim edges even and bind with self-made or purchased binding to finish. ❖

Lost in Space

BY JUDITH SANDSTROM

Many years ago, a television show called *Lost in Space* told the story of a family who landed on another planet and could not get home. That show inspired the quiltmaker to create this quilt. If you prefer the traditional method—using templates—those instructions are here. If, however, you prefer quick piecing methods, you might want to try the instructions on page 84. Whichever instructions you use, you won't get lost in space making this delightful wall hanging.

Lost in Space

Project Specifications
Quilt Size: 28½" x 43½"
Block Size: 7½" x 7½"
Number of Blocks: 15

Fabric & Batting
- ¼ yard each rust, blue, yellow and purple prints
- ⅓ yard multicolored print
- ⅜ yard each green and pink prints
- 1 yard black print
- Backing 33" x 48"
- Low-loft batting 33" x 48"
- 4½ yards self-made or purchased binding

Supplies & Tools
- Neutral color all-purpose thread
- White quilting thread

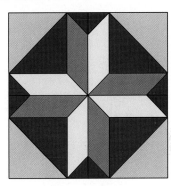

Lost in Space
7 1/2" x 7 1/2" Block

- Basic sewing supplies and tools, rotary cutter, ruler and cutting mat

Traditional Method

1. Prepare templates using pattern pieces given. Cut as directed on each piece for one block; repeat for 15 blocks.

2. To piece one block, sew a pink print A to a black print A along the diagonal; repeat for four A units.

Lost in Space

Lost in Space
Placement Diagram
28 1/2" x 43 1/2"

3. Using yellow and purple print B and BR pieces; sew a C triangle to one end of each piece as shown in Figure 1. Sew a B-C and BR-C unit to the A unit as shown in Figure 2 to complete one quarter of the block; repeat for four units.

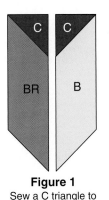

Figure 1
Sew a C triangle to
1 end of each piece.

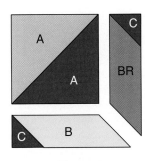

Figure 2
Sew a B-C and BR-C unit
to the A unit as shown.

4. Join four pieced units to complete one block as shown in Figure 3; repeat for 15 blocks making eight blocks with the pink/yellow/purple color combination and seven blocks with the green/blue/rust color combination.

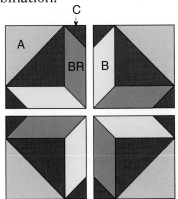

Figure 3
Join 4 pieced units to complete 1 block.

5. Join two pink/yellow/purple blocks with one green/blue/rust block to make a row; repeat for three rows. Press seams in one direction.

6. Join two green/blue/rust blocks with one pink/yellow/purple block to make a row; repeat for two rows.

7. Join pieced rows referring to the Placement Diagram; press seams in one direction.

8. Cut two strips each black print 2" x 23" and 2" x 41". Sew the shorter srtrips to the top and bottom and the longer strips to opposite sides; press seams toward strips.

9. Cut two strips each multicolored print 2" x 29" and 2" x 41". Sew the longer strips to opposite sides and shorter strips to the top and bottom; press seams toward strips.

10. Sandwich batting between completed top and prepared backing piece; pin or baste layers together to hold flat for quilting.

11. Quilt as desired by hand or machine. *Note: The quilt shown was hand-quilted in the ditch of seams*

Lost in Space

using white quilting thread. When quilting is complete, trim edges even; remove pins or basting.

12. Bind edges with self-made or purchased binding to finish.

Quick Method

1. From black print, cut three strips 3⅝" by fabric width and eight strips 1¼" by fabric width. Subcut the 3⅝" strips into 3⅝" squares. Cut 30 squares on one diagonal to make 60 A triangles.

2. From each of the rust, blue, yellow and purple prints, cut two strips 2½" by fabric width.

3. From both the green and pink prints, cut two strips 3⅝" by fabric width. Subcut the 3⅝" strips into 3⅝" squares. Cut 16 pink print squares and 14 green print squares on one diagonal to make A triangles. You will need 32 pink print and 28 green print A triangles.

4. Sew a 2½" colored print strip to a 1¼" black print strip right sides together along length; press seams open.

5. Cut each strip at a 45-degree angle in 1½" intervals, cutting all blue or purple/black strips in one direction and all rust or yellow/black strips in the

opposite direction as shown in Figure 4. *Note: If you have a problem cutting the angle, cut out the B and C templates; tape together at seam lines and use template to cut strips.*

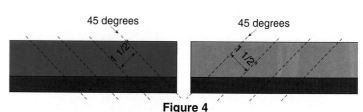

Figure 4
Cut each strip at a 45-degree angle in 1 1/2" intervals, cutting all blue or purple/black strips in 1 direction and rust or yellow/black strips in the opposite direction.

6. Stitch each rust segment to a blue segment and each yellow segment to a purple segment as shown in Figure 5; press seams open. Cut across each unit at the seam points where the color and black meet as shown in Figure 6. Trim off the fabric points at the pointed end of each unit as shown in Figure 7.

Figure 5
Stitch each rust segment to a blue segment and each yellow segment to a purple segment.

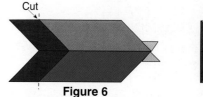

Figure 6
Cut across each unit at the seam points where the color and black meet.

Figure 7
Trim off the fabric points at the pointed end of each unit.

7. Sew a pink print A to a black print A along the diagonal to make an A unit; repeat with all pink print and green print A triangles.

8. Join two same-fabric segments from step 6 as shown in Figure 8; repeat with all segments. Set a green A unit into each rust/blue unit as shown in Figure 9. Repeat with pink A units and purple/yellow units.

Figure 8
Join 2 same-fabric segments.

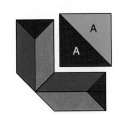

Figure 9
Set in an A unit.

9. Join same-fabric pieced units as shown in Figure 10 to complete one block; repeat to make 15 blocks as in step 4 for Traditional Method.

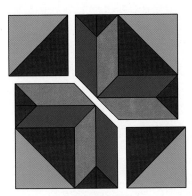

Figure 10
Join same-fabric pieced units.

10. Complete quilt as for Traditional Method. ❖

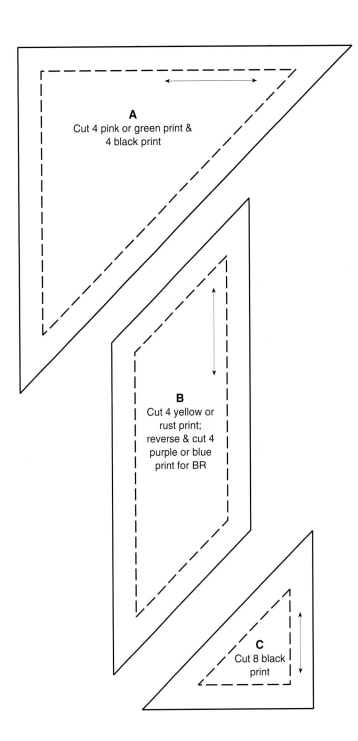

A
Cut 4 pink or green print &
4 black print

B
Cut 4 yellow or
rust print;
reverse & cut 4
purple or blue
print for BR

C
Cut 8 black
print

Masks From the Past

BY LUCY A. FAZELY

Finding fabric that looked like wood block prints inspired this quilt designer to make a quilt that reflects ancient cultures. Using fusible web and the machine-appliqué buttonhole-stitch makes this quilt quick to create. This striking quilt is a work of art that could be displayed in a museum.

Masks From the Past

Masks From the Past
Placement Diagram
32" x 32"

Masks From the Past

Project Specifications

Quilt Size: 32" x 32"

Block Size: 6" x 6", 6" x 8" and 8" x 8"

Number of Blocks: 4 small, 2 each remaining sizes

Fabric & Batting

- 8 squares different wood block prints 8" x 8" for masks
- ½ yard tan solid
- 1 yard total wood block prints for bordering squares
- Backing 36" x 36"
- Batting 36" x 36"
- 4 yards self-made or purchased binding

Supplies & Tools

- Black all-purpose thread
- Clear nylon monofilament
- 1 yard fusible web
- 1 yard fabric stabilizer
- Basic sewing tools and supplies, rotary cutter, ruler and cutting mat

Instructions

1. Cut the following from tan solid: four 6½" x 6½" squares; two 6½" x 8½" rectangles and two 8½" x 8½" squares.

2. Cut 164 squares from various wood block prints 2½" x 2½".

3. Cut eight squares fusible web 7" x 7" and eight squares fabric stabilizer 8" x 8".

4. Bond a 7" x 7" square fusible web to the wrong side of each 8" x 8" wood block print square for masks.

5. Prepare templates for each mask shape using patterns given. Trace each mask shape onto the paper side of one wood block print square.

6. Cut out each shape on traced lines; remove paper backing.

7. Center and fuse mask shapes to the tan solid squares and rectangles referring to the Placement Diagram for placing masks on the correct-size background pieces.

8. Attach fabric stabilizer to the wrong side of each fused square. Using black all-purpose thread, machine buttonhole-stitch around each shape and

Masks From the Past

on inside detail lines. When appliqué is complete, remove fabric stabilizer.

9. Join the 2½" x 2½" block print squares in units as shown in Figure 1.

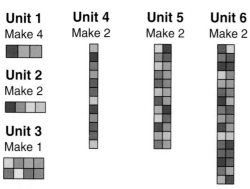

Figure 1
Join the 2 1/2" x 2 1/2" squares in units as shown.

10. Join two 6½" x 6½" appliquéd blocks with two Unit 1 strips and a 6½" x 8½" block to make a vertical row as shown in Figure 2; press seams in one direction. Repeat for two rows.

Figure 2
Join two 6 1/2" x 6 1/2" appliquéd blocks with 2 Unit 1 strips and a 6 1/2" x 8 1/2" block to make a vertical row.

11. Join the two 8½" x 8½" blocks with a Unit 3 strip as shown in Figure 3. Sew Unit 2 to the top and bottom to complete a vertical row.

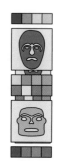

Figure 3
Join the two 8 1/2" x 8 1/2" blocks with a Unit 3 strip as shown; sew Unit 2 to the top and bottom to complete a vertical row.

12. Join the three vertical rows with Unit 4 strips as shown in Figure 4; sew Unit 5 to each vertical side and Unit 6 to the top and bottom to complete the pieced top, again referring to Figure 4.

Figure 4
Join the 3 vertical rows with Unit 4 strips as shown; sew Unit 5 to each vertical side and Unit 6 to the top and bottom to complete the pieced top.

13. Sandwich batting between completed top and prepared backing; pin or baste layers together to hold flat.

14. Quilt as desired by hand or machine; remove pins or basting. *Note: The quilt shown was machine-quilted in the ditch of seams and around* *mask shapes using clear nylon monofilament in the top of the machine and all-purpose thread in the bobbin.*

15. When quilting is complete, trim edges even; remove pins or basting. Bind edges with self-made or purchased binding to finish. ❖

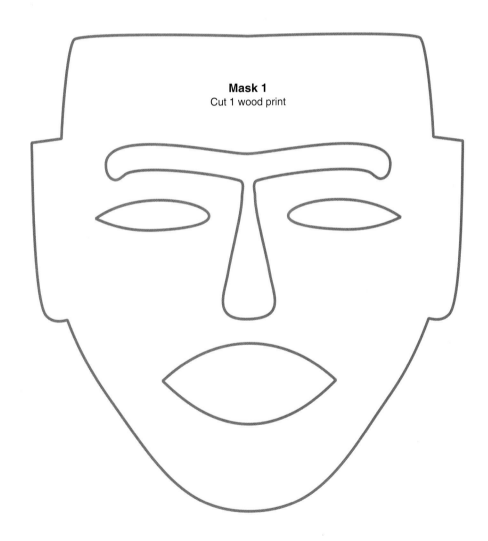

Mask 1
Cut 1 wood print

Masks From the Past

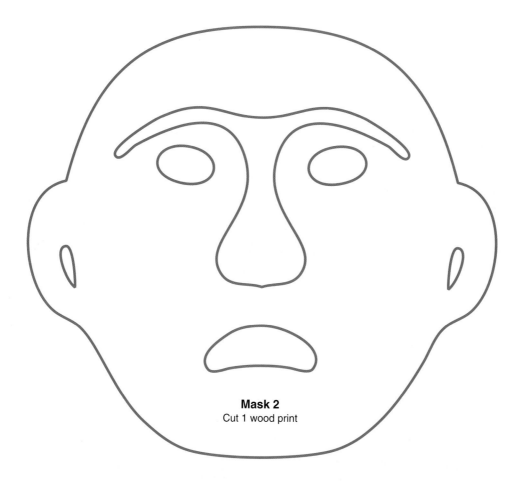

Mask 2
Cut 1 wood print

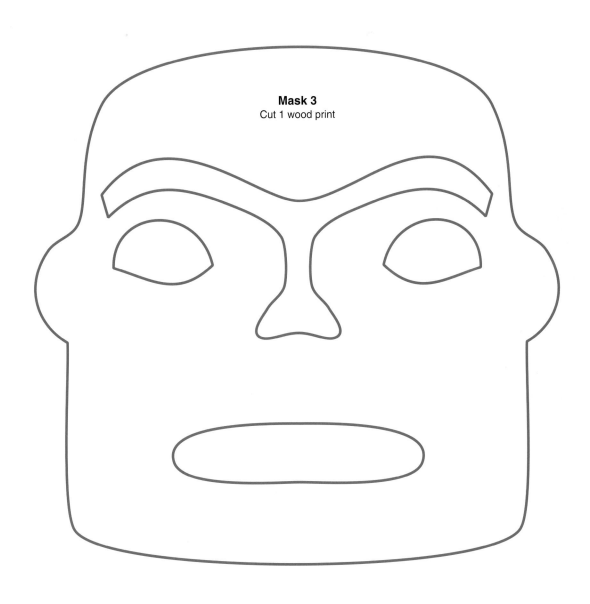

Mask 3
Cut 1 wood print

Masks From the Past

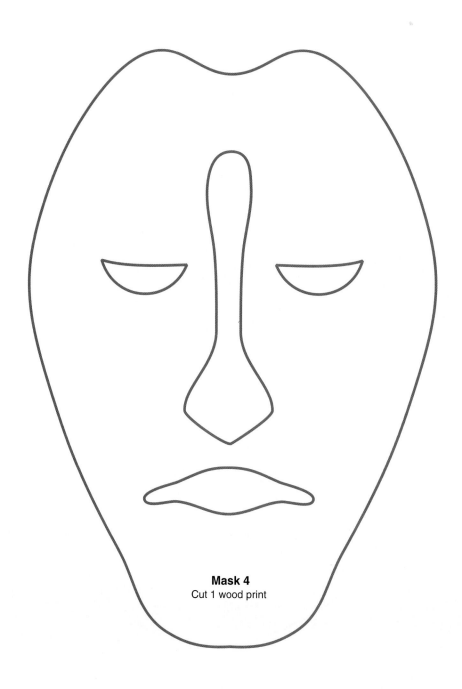

Mask 4
Cut 1 wood print

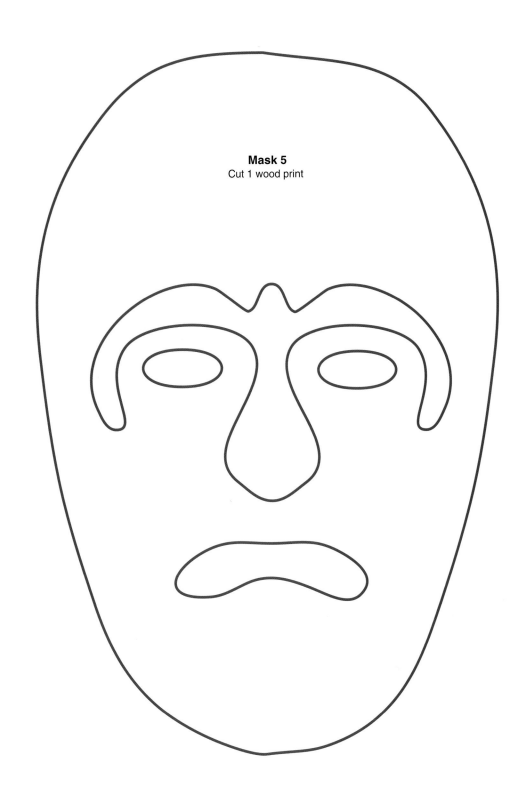

Mask 5
Cut 1 wood print

Masks From the Past

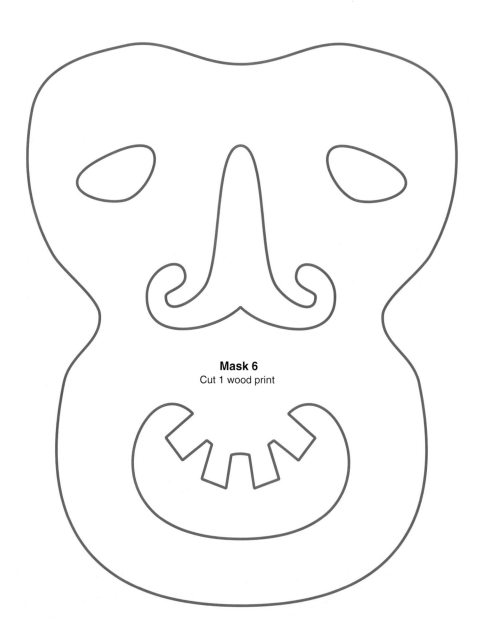

Mask 6
Cut 1 wood print

Mask 7
Cut 1 wood print

Mask 8
Cut 1 wood print

Spools

BY PATSY MORELAND

This small wall hanging announces the owner to be a sewer and that spools of thread are among her favorite things. The quilt is very easy to piece because it uses simple triangles and squares. If you enjoy using templates to create your finished quilt, follow the instructions for the traditional method. If, however, you like to work quickly, you'll want to follow the quick method, which will leave you plenty of time for all of your other sewing projects.

Spools

Project Specifications

Quilt Size: 36" x 42"

Block Size: 6" x 6"

Number of Blocks: 20

Fabric & Batting

- ¼ yard each lime green, purple, orange, forest green, burgundy and rust mottleds
- ⅜ yard light brown mottled
- ½ yard white-on-white print
- 1 yard dark brown mottled
- Backing 40" x 46"
- Batting 40" x 46"
- 4¾ yards self-made or purchased binding

Supplies & Tools

- Neutral color all-purpose thread
- Gold machine-quilting thread

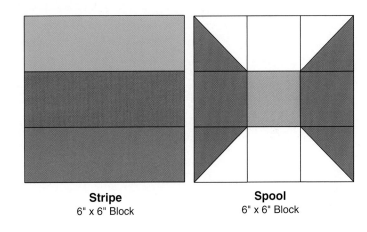

Stripe
6" x 6" Block

Spool
6" x 6" Block

- Basic sewing tools and supplies

Traditional Method

1. Prepare templates using pattern pieces given; cut as directed on each piece for one block.

2. To piece one Spool block, sew a white-on-white print A to a dark brown mottled A along the diagonal; repeat for four A units.

Spools

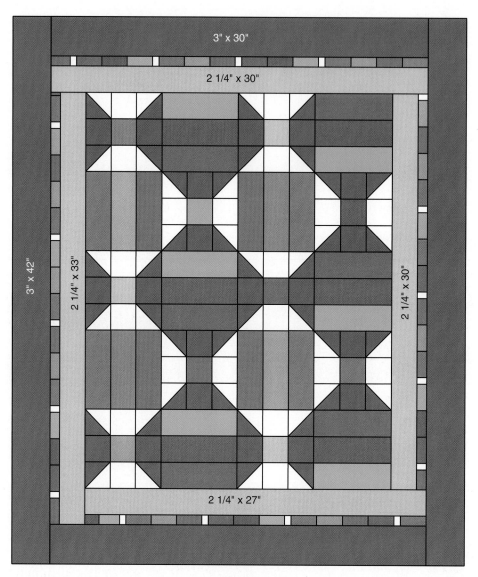

Spools
Placement Diagram
36" x 42"

3. Arrange the A units in rows with one bright mottled and two each white-on-white print and dark brown mottled B squares referring to Figure 1. Join pieces in rows; join the rows to complete one block. Repeat for 10 blocks.

Figure 1
Arrange the A units in rows with
1 bright mottled and 2 each
white-on-white print and dark
brown mottled B squares.

4. To piece one Stripe block, join three C pieces in any color order as shown in Figure 2; repeat for 10 blocks in different color combinations referring to the Placement Diagram.

Figure 2
To piece 1 Stripe block,
join 3 C pieces in any
color order as shown.

5. Join two Spool and two Stripe blocks to make a row referring to the Placement Diagram for positioning of blocks; repeat for five rows. Press seams in one direction. Join the rows referring to the Placement Diagram to complete the pieced center. Press seams in one direction.

6. Cut one strip each light brown mottled 2¾" x 27½" and 2¾" x 33½" and two strips 2¾" x 30½".

7. Cut one strip each lime green, purple, orange, forest green, burgundy and rust mottleds 2½" by fabric width; cut each strip in half across width.

8. Cut two strips white-on-white print 1" by fabric width; cut one strip in half across width.

9. Join the colored strips in groups of two, three or four along length with right sides together to make four pieced strips. Join two pieced strips with a white-on-white print strip; press seams in one direction. Repeat for two strip sets.

10. Cut the strip sets into 1¼" segments as shown in Figure 3.

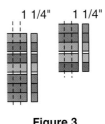

Figure 3
Cut the strip
sets into 1¼"
segments.

11. Cut the remaining white-on-white print strip into 1¼" segments. Join the pieced segments with white-on-white print segments to make one long strip. *Note: This strip needs to be at least 125" long.*

Spools

12. Sew any 2¾" light brown mottled strip to the long pieced strip; press seam toward wider strip. Trim excess pieced strip to fit the wider strip as shown in Figure 4; repeat with remaining light brown mottled strips.

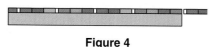

Figure 4
Trim excess pieced strip to fit the wider strip as shown.

13. Sew a 30½" pieced strip to one long side of the pieced center; press seam toward strip. Continue to add the strips to the sides in a clockwise order referring to the Placement Diagram for positioning of strips; press seams toward strips.

14. Cut two strips each 3½" x 30½" and 3½" x 42½" dark brown mottled. Sew the shorter strips to opposite short sides and longer strips to the remaining long sides of the pieced center; press seams toward strips.

15. Sandwich batting between completed top and prepared backing piece; pin or baste to hold layers together.

16. Quilt as desired by hand or machine *Note: The quilt shown was machine-quilted using gold machine-quilting thread in a meandering pattern.*

17. When quilting is complete, trim edges even and remove pins or basting. Bind edges with self-made or purchased binding to finish.

Quick Method

1. Cut two strips each white-on-white print and dark brown mottled 2⅞" by fabric width. Subcut strips into 2⅞" square segments. You will need 20 square segments of each color.

2. Cut each square in half on one diagonal to make A triangles. Sew a dark triangle to a light triangle; repeat for 40 units.

3. Cut two strips each white-on-white print and dark brown mottled 2½" by fabric width; subcut strips into 2½" square segments to make 20 B squares of each color.

4. Cut one strip each lime green, purple, orange, forest green, burgundy and rust mottleds 2½" by fabric width. Randomly cut 10 squares from strips for bright mottled B squares.

5. Join A units and B squares as in step 3 for Traditional Method to complete 10 Spool blocks.

6. Join remainder of three strips in random color order with right sides together along length; repeat

for two strip sets. Press seams in one direction.

7. Cut each strip set into five 6½" segments to complete 10 Stripe blocks.

8. Complete the quilt referring to the Traditional Method steps 5–17. ❖

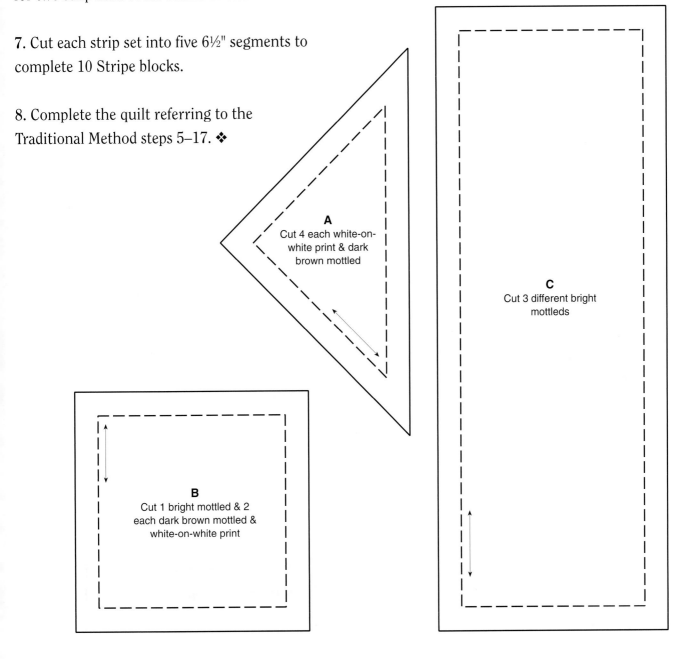

A
Cut 4 each white-on-white print & dark brown mottled

C
Cut 3 different bright mottleds

B
Cut 1 bright mottled & 2 each dark brown mottled & white-on-white print

Crossed T's

BY CHRISTINE CARLSON

The simple Crossed T's square
creates a secondary design—an
example of crosspatching in which
two or more different block designs
emerge when the same blocks are
set side by side. Using quick-piecing
methods and the A-E Bias Square
template, this quilt can be completed
quickly and will be admired for years.

Crossed T's

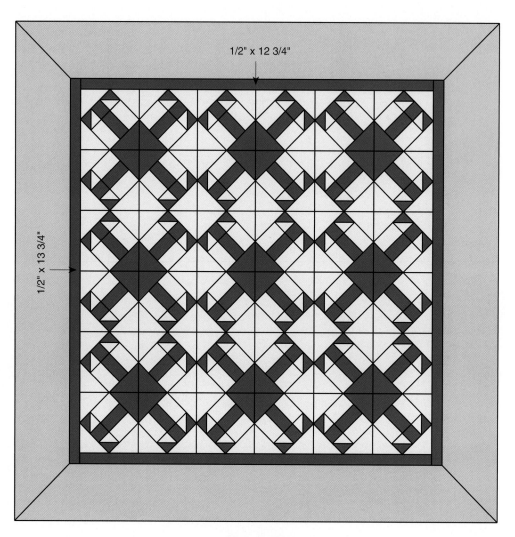

1/2" x 12 3/4"

1/2" x 13 3/4"

Crossed T's
Placement Diagram
17 3/4" x 17 3/4"
(includes binding)

Crossed T's

Project Specifications

Quilt Size: 17¾" x 17¾" (includes binding)
Block Size: 2⅛" x 2⅛"
Number of Blocks: 36

Fabric & Batting

- ½ yard each dark green and light green prints
- 1 fat quarter pink floral
- Backing 20" x 20"
- Batting 20" x 20"
- 2¼ yards self-made or purchased binding

Supplies & Tools

- Neutral color all-purpose thread
- White hand-quilting thread
- Baby Bias Square ruler
- Basic sewing tools and supplies and rotary-cutting equipment

Instructions

Note: A ¼" seam allowance is included in all measurements. Except for sashing and border seams, press all seams open as shown by small arrows and trim to ⅛" if desired.

1. Cut two rectangles dark green print 11" x 18" for A; repeat with light green print for E. Layer one each A and E rectangles right sides together. Cut

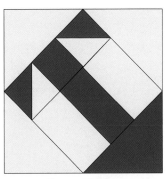

Crossed T's
2 1/8" x 2 1/8" Block

the layered rectangles in four 1⅛" x 15½" strips as shown in Figure 1; repeat.

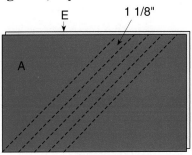

Figure 1
Cut the layered rectangles in four
1 1/8" x 15 1/2" strips as shown.

2. Sew an A strip to an E strip with right sides together along length to make an A/E bias set; repeat for eight sets.

3. Cut 1" x 1" bias squares from each set to make 72 A-E bias squares as shown in Figure 2.
Note: Use the Baby Bias Square ruler or use the template given.

Figure 2
Cut 1" x 1" bias squares
from each set to make
A-E bias squares.

Crossed T's

4. Cut 36 squares dark green print 1" x 1" for B.

5. Sew an A-E bias square to opposite sides of a B square as shown in Figure 3; repeat for 36 A/E-B units.

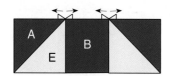

Figure 3
Sew an A-E bias square to
opposite sides of a B square.

6. Cut four strips dark green print 1" x 16" for C; repeat for eight strips light green print for F. Sew a C strip between two F strips with right sides together along length; press. Repeat for four F-C-F sets. Subcut sets into 1½" segments as shown in Figure 4; repeat for 36 F-C-F units.

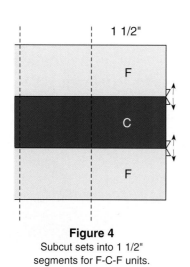

1 1/2"

Figure 4
Subcut sets into 1 1/2"
segments for F-C-F units.

7. Sew an F-C-F unit to the bottom of an A/E-B unit as shown in Figure 5; repeat for 36 units.

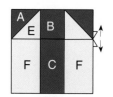

Figure 5
Sew an F-C-F unit to
the bottom of an A/E-B
unit as shown.

8. Cut 18 squares dark green print 1¹⁵⁄₁₆" x 1¹⁵⁄₁₆" for G; repeat for 54 light green print H squares. Cut each square in half on one diagonal to make 36 G and 108 H triangles.

9. Sew a G triangle to the F-C-F end of a pieced unit as shown in Figure 6. Sew an H triangle to all three remaining sides to complete one Crossed T's block as shown in Figure 7; press. Repeat for 36 blocks.

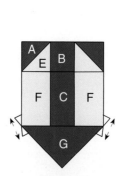

Figure 6
Sew a G triangle to
the F-C-F end of a
pieced unit.

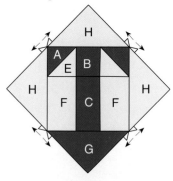

Figure 7
Sew an H triangle to
all 3 remaining sides
to complete 1
Crossed T's block.

10. Arrange six blocks to make a row as shown in Figure 8; repeat for six rows. Press seams open.

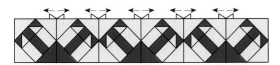

Figure 8
Arrange 6 blocks to make a row.

11. Join the rows referring to the Placement Diagram for positioning of rows; press seams open.

12. Cut two strips each 1" x 13¼" and 1" x 14¼" dark green print. Sew the shorter strips to the top and bottom and longer strips to opposite sides; press seams toward strips.

13. Cut four strips 2¼" x 20". Center and sew a strip to each side of the pieced center, mitering corners. Trim seam allowance and press seams toward strips.

14. Sandwich batting between completed top and prepared backing piece; pin or baste to hold layers together.

15. Quilt as desired by hand or machine. *Note: The quilt shown was hand-quilted in the ditch of seams using white quilting thread.*

16. When quilting is complete, remove basting or pins. Trim edges even. Bind with self-made or purchased binding to finish. ❖

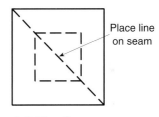

Place line on seam

A-E Bias Square

French Country

BY MICHELE CRAWFORD

Hang this quilt on your wall, and you will surely feel that you are in the French countryside on a bright summer afternoon. The combination of the blue and yellow fabrics gives this pretty quilt a special charm and warmth that will bring a smile to the face of anyone who experiences this petite beauty.

French Country

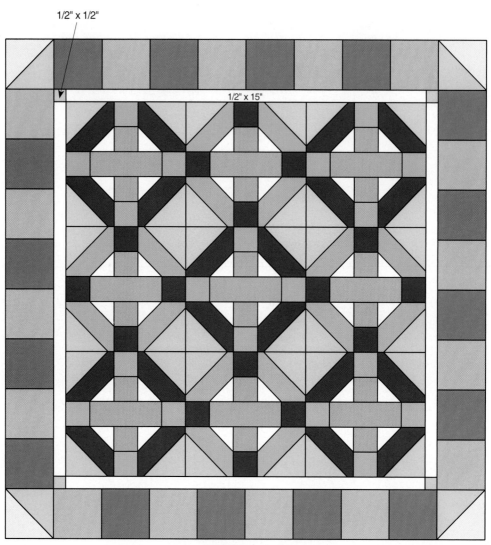

1/2" x 1/2"

1/2" x 15"

French Country
Placement Diagram
20" x 20"

French Country

Project Specifications

Quilt Size: 20" x 20"

Block Size: 5" x 5"

Number of Blocks: 9

Fabric & Batting

- ⅙ yard each royal blue and yellow prints
- ⅛ yard each light blue, yellow/blue, large floral and white/blue prints
- ⅛ yard blue plaid
- ⅞ yard white-on-white print
- ¾ yard quilter's fleece

Supplies & Tools

- 1 spool each white, blue and yellow all-purpose thread
- 1 spool each white, navy and yellow quilting thread
- Clear nylon monofilament
- 1 package white wide bias tape
- Basic sewing tools and supplies

Instructions

Note: Use a ¼" seam unless otherwise indicated. Sew pieces with right sides together and raw edges even. Press seam allowance toward the darkest fabric.

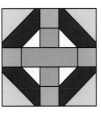

Make 5

Block A
5" x 5" Block

Make 4

Block B
5" x 5" Block

1. Prepare template for piece A using pattern piece given; cut as directed on piece.

2. Cut the following: yellow print—18 squares 2½" x 2½"; light blue print—20 squares 1½" x 1½" for LB; royal blue print—16 squares 1½" x 1½" for RB; yellow/blue print—nine 1½" x 3½" rectangles for YB and 18 squares 1½" x 1½" for YBS; white-on-white print—18 squares 1⅞" x 1⅞".

3. Cut 2½" x 2½" yellow print squares on one diagonal to make 36 Y triangles. Cut 1⅞" x 1⅞" squares white-on-white print on one diagonal to make 36 W triangles.

4. Join pieces referring to Figure 1 to make one A Block; repeat for five blocks.

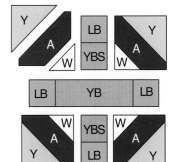

Figure 1
Join pieces as shown to make Block A.

French Country

5. Join pieces referring to Figure 2 to make one B Block; repeat for four blocks.

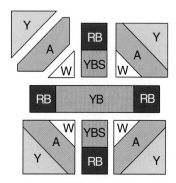

Figure 2
Join pieces as shown
to make Block B.

6. Join two A Blocks with one B Block to make a row as shown in Figure 3; repeat for two rows.

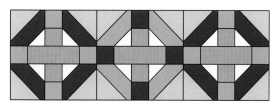

Figure 3
Join 2 A Blocks with 1 B Block to make a row.

7. Join two B Blocks with one A Block to make a row as shown in Figure 4.

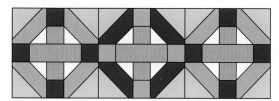

Figure 4
Join 2 B Blocks with 1 A Block to make a row.

8. Join block rows to complete pieced center as shown in Figure 5; press.

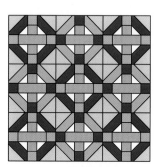

Figure 5
Join rows to complete pieced center.

9. Cut four strips white-on-white print 1" x 15½" and four squares yellow print 1" x 1". Sew a white-on-white print strip to two opposite sides of the pieced center; press. Sew a yellow print square to each end of the remaining two white-on-white print strips. Sew a strip to each remaining side; press.

10. Cut 16 squares each blue plaid (P) and large floral print (F) 2½" x 2½". Join four each F and P squares to make a strip as shown in Figure 6; repeat for four strips. Sew a strip to two opposite sides of the pieced center; press.

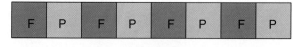

Figure 6
Join 4 F and P squares to make a row.

11. Cut two squares each yellow (Y) and white/blue floral prints (WB) 2⅞" x 2⅞". Cut each square in half on one diagonal to make triangles. Sew Y to WB to make a triangle/square; repeat for four units.

12. Sew a Y-WB unit to each end of the remaining two border strips as shown in Figure 7. Sew a strip to each of the remaining sides; press.

Figure 7
Sew Y-WB units to each end of strip.

13. Cut one piece each quilter's fleece and white-on-white print backing 24" x 24". Sandwich fleece between backing and pieced top; pin or baste layers together to hold flat.

14. Hand-quilt ¼" in from seams on A and an X in the royal blue print squares using yellow quilting thread. Hand-quilt down the center of the white-on-white border strips using navy quilting thread. Hand-quilt diagonally through each square in the pieced border using white quilting thread.

15. Machine-quilt in the ditch of border seams using clear nylon monofilament in the top of the machine and white all-purpose thread in the bobbin.

16. When quilting is complete, topstitch ⅛" around outside edges; trim edges even.

17. Bind edges with white wide bias tape, mitering corners and overlapping ends. Turn binding to backside; hand-stitch in place to finish. ❖

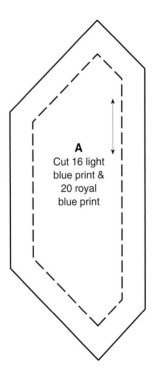

A
Cut 16 light
blue print &
20 royal
blue print

General Instructions

Quiltmaking Basics

Materials & Supplies

Fabrics
Fabric Choices. Quilts and quilted projects combine fabrics of many types. Use same-fiber-content fabrics when making quilted items, if possible.

Buying Fabrics. One hundred percent cotton fabrics are recommended for making quilts. Choose colors similar to those used in the quilts shown or colors of your own preference. Most quilt designs depend more on contrast of values than on the colors used to create the design.

Preparing the Fabric for Use. Fabrics may be prewashed depending on your preference. Whether you prewash or not, be sure your fabrics are colorfast and won't run onto each other when washed after use.

Fabric Grain. Fabrics are woven with threads going in a crosswise and lengthwise direction. The threads cross at right angles—the more threads per inch, the stronger the fabric.

The crosswise threads will stretch a little. The lengthwise threads will not stretch at all. Cutting the fabric at a 45-degree angle to the crosswise and lengthwise threads produces a bias edge which stretches a great deal when pulled (Figure 1).

If templates are given with patterns in this book, pay careful attention to the grain lines marked with arrows. These arrows indicate that the piece should be placed on the lengthwise grain with the arrow running on one thread. Although it is not necessary to examine the fabric and find a thread to match to, it is important to try to place the arrow with the lengthwise grain of the fabric (Figure 2).

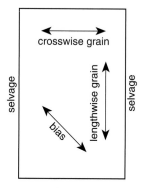

Figure 1
Drawing shows lengthwise, crosswise and bias threads.

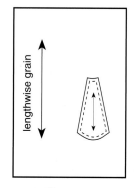

Figure 2
Place the template with marked arrow on the lengthwise grain of the fabric.

Thread
For most piecing, good-quality cotton or cotton-covered polyester is the thread of choice. Inexpensive polyester threads are not recommended because they can cut the fibers of cotton fabrics.

Choose a color thread that will match or blend with the fabrics in your quilt. For projects pieced with dark and light color fabrics choose a neutral thread color, such as a medium gray, as a compromise between colors. Test by pulling a sample seam.

Batting
Batting is the material used to give a quilt loft or thickness. It also adds warmth.

Batting size is listed in inches for each pattern to reflect the size needed to complete the quilt according to the instructions. Purchase the size large enough to cut the size you need for the quilt of your choice.

Some qualities to look for in batting are drapability, resistance to fiber migration, loft and softness.

Tools & Equipment

There are few truly essential tools and little equipment required for quiltmaking. Basics include needles (hand-sewing and quilting betweens), pins (long, thin, sharp pins are best), sharp scissors or shears, a thimble, template materials (plastic or cardboard), marking tools (chalk marker, water-erasable pen and a No. 2 pencil are a few) and a quilting frame or hoop. For piecing and/or quilting by machine, add a sewing machine to the list.

Other sewing basics such as a seam ripper, pincushion, measuring tape and an iron are also necessary. For choosing colors or quilting designs for your quilt, or for designing your own quilt, it is helpful to have on hand graph paper, tracing paper, colored pencils or markers and a ruler.

For making strip-pieced quilts, a rotary cutter, mat and specialty rulers are often used. We recommend an ergonomic rotary cutter, a large self-healing mat and several rulers. If you can choose only one size, a 6" x 24" marked in ⅛" or ¼" increments is recommended.

Construction Methods

Traditional Templates. While some quilt instructions in this book use rotary-cut strips and quick sewing methods, many patterns require a template. Templates are like the pattern pieces used to sew a garment. They are used to cut the fabric pieces that make up the quilt top. There are two types—templates that include a ¼" seam allowance and those that don't.

Choose the template material and the pattern. Transfer the pattern shapes to the template material with a sharp No. 2 lead pencil. Write the pattern name, piece letter or number, grain line and number to cut for one block or whole quilt on each piece as shown in Figure 3.

Some patterns require a reversed piece (Figure 4). These patterns are labeled with an R after the piece letter; for example, B and BR. To reverse a template, first cut it with the labeled side up and then with the labeled side down. Compare these to the right and left fronts of a blouse. When making a garment, you accomplish reversed pieces when cutting the pattern on two layers of fabric placed with right sides together. This can be done when cutting templates as well.

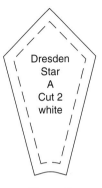

Figure 3
Mark each template with the pattern name and piece identification.

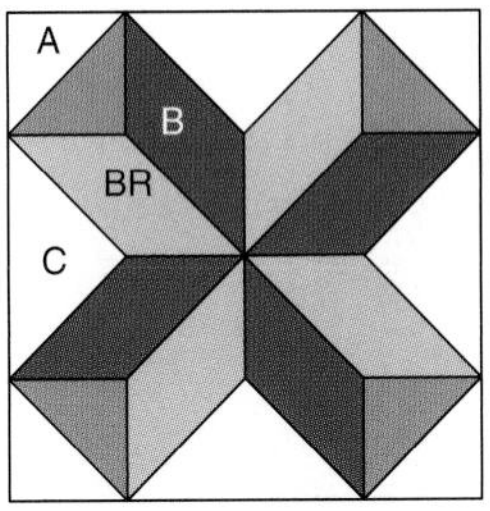

Figure 4
This pattern uses reversed pieces.

If cutting one layer of fabric at a time, first trace the template onto the backside of the fabric with the marked side down; turn the template over with the marked side up to make reverse pieces.

Hand-Piecing Basics. When hand-piecing it is easier to begin with templates that do not include the ¼" seam allowance. Place the template on the wrong side of the fabric, lining up the marked grain line with lengthwise or crosswise fabric grain. If the piece does not have to be reversed, place with labeled side up. Trace around shape; move, leaving ½" between the shapes, and mark again.

When you have marked the appropriate number of pieces, cut out pieces, leaving ¼" beyond marked line all around each piece.

To join two units, place the patches with right sides together. Stick a pin in at the beginning of the seam through both fabric patches, matching the beginning points (Figure 5); for hand-piecing, the seam begins on the traced line, not at the edge of the fabric (see Figure 6).

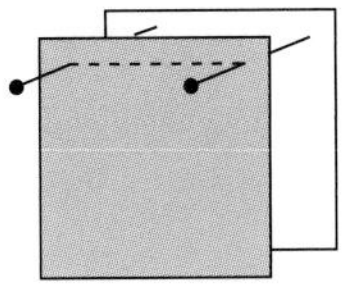

Figure 5
Stick a pin through fabrics to match the beginning of the seam.

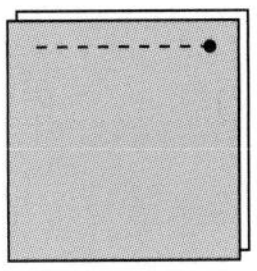

Figure 6
Begin hand-piecing at seam, not at the edge of the fabric. Continue stitching along seam line.

General Instructions

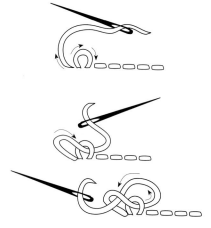

Thread a sharp needle; knot one strand of the thread at the end. Remove the pin and insert the needle in the hole; make a short stitch and then a backstitch right over the first stitch. Continue making short stitches with several stitches on the needle at one time. As you stitch, check the back piece often to assure accurate stitching on the seam line. Take a stitch at the end of the seam; backstitch and knot at the same time as shown in Figure 7. Seams on hand-pieced fabric patches may be finger-pressed toward the darker fabric.

Figure 7
Make a loop in backstitch to make a knot.

To sew units together, pin fabric patches together, matching seams. Sew as above except where seams meet; at these intersections, backstitch, go through seam to next piece and backstitch again to secure seam joint.

Not all pieced blocks can be stitched with straight seams or in rows. Some patterns require set-in pieces. To begin a set-in seam, pin one side of the square to the proper side of the star point with right sides together, matching corners. Start stitching at the seam line on the outside point; stitch on the marked seam line to the end of the seam line at the center referring to Figure 8.

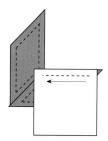

Figure 8
To set a square into a diamond point, match seams and stitch from outside edge to center.

Bring around the adjacent side and pin to the next star point, matching seams. Continue the stitching line from the adjacent seam through corners and to the outside edge of the square as shown in Figure 9.

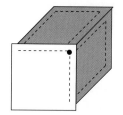

Figure 9
Continue stitching the adjacent side of the square to the next diamond shape in 1 seam from center to outside as shown.

Machine-Piecing. If making templates, include the ¼" seam allowance on the template for machine-piecing. Place template on the wrong side of the fabric as for hand-piecing except butt pieces against one another when tracing.

Set machine on 2.5 or 12–15 stitches per inch. Join pieces as for hand-piecing for set-in seams; but for other straight seams, begin and end sewing at the end of the fabric patch sewn as shown in Figure 10. No backstitching is necessary when machine-stitching.

Figure 10
Begin machine-piecing at the end of the piece, not at the end of the seam.

Join units as for hand-piecing referring to the piecing diagrams where needed. Chain piecing (Figure 11—sewing several like units before sewing other units) saves time by eliminating beginning and ending stitches.

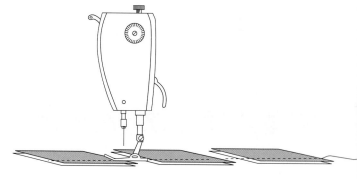

Figure 11
Units may be chain-pieced to save time.

When joining machine-pieced units, match seams against each other with seam allowances pressed in opposite directions to reduce bulk and make perfect matching of seams possible (Figure 12).

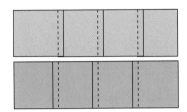

Figure 12
Sew machine-pieced units with seams pressed in opposite directions.

Quick-Cutting. Templates can be completely eliminated when using a rotary cutter with a plastic ruler and mat to cut fabric strips.

When rotary-cutting strips, straighten raw edges of fabric by folding fabric in fourths across the width as shown in Figure 13. Press down flat; place ruler on fabric square with edge of fabric and make one cut from the folded edge to the outside edge. If strips are not straightened, a wavy strip will result as shown in Figure 14.

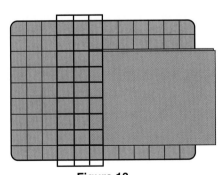

Figure 13
Fold fabric and straighten as shown.

Figure 14
Wavy strips result if fabric is not straightened before cutting.

Always cut away from your body, holding the ruler firmly with the non-cutting hand. Keep fingers away from the edge of the ruler as it is easy for the rotary cutter to slip and jump over the edge of the ruler if cutting is not properly done.

If a square is required for the pattern, it can be subcut from a strip as shown in Figure 15.

Figure 15
If cutting squares, cut proper-width strip into same-width segments. Here, a 2" strip is cut into 2" segments to create 2" squares. These squares finish at 1 1/2" when sewn.

If you need right triangles with the straight grain on the short sides, you can use the same method, but you need to figure out how wide to cut the strip. Measure the finished size of one short side of the triangle. Add $\frac{7}{8}$" to this size for seam allowance. Cut fabric strips this width; cut the strips into the same increment to create squares. Cut the squares on the diagonal to produce triangles. For example, if you need a triangle with a 2" finished height, cut the strips $2\frac{7}{8}$" by the width of the fabric. Cut the strips into $2\frac{7}{8}$" squares. Cut each square on the diagonal to produce the correct-size triangle with the grain on the short sides (Figure 16).

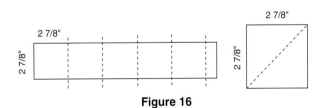

Figure 16
Cut 2" (finished size) triangles from 2 7/8" squares as shown.

Triangles sewn together to make squares are called half-square triangles or triangle/squares. When joined, the triangle/square unit has the straight of grain on all outside edges of the block.

Another method of making triangle/squares is shown in Figure 17. Layer two squares with right sides together; draw a diagonal line through the center. Stitch ¼" on both sides of the line.

General Instructions

Cut apart on the drawn line to reveal two stitched triangle/squares.

Figure 17
Mark a diagonal line on the square; stitch
1/4" on each side of the line. Cut on line
to reveal stitched triangle/squares.

If you need triangles with the straight of grain on the diagonal, such as for fill-in triangles on the outside edges of a diagonal-set quilt, the procedure is a bit different.

To make these triangles, a square is cut on both diagonals; thus, the straight of grain is on the longest or diagonal side (Figure 18). To figure out the size to cut the square, add 1¼" to the needed finished size of the longest side of the triangle. For example, if you need a triangle with a 12" finished diagonal, cut a 13¼" square.

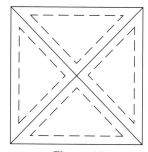

Figure 18
Add 1 1/4" to the finished size of the
longest side of the triangle needed
and cut on both diagonals to make a
quarter-square triangle.

If templates are given, use their measurments to cut fabric strips to correspond with that measurement. The template may be used on the strip to cut pieces quickly. Strip cutting works best for squares, triangles, rectangles and diamonds. Odd-shaped templates are difficult to cut in multiple layers or using a rotary cutter.

Quick-Piecing Method.

Lay pieces to be joined under the presser foot of the sewing machine right sides together. Sew an exact ¼" seam allowance to the end of the piece; place another unit right next to the first one and continue sewing, adding a piece after every stitched piece, until all of the pieces are used up (Figure 19).

Figure 19
Sew pieces together in a chain.

When sewing is finished, cut threads joining the pieces apart. Press seam toward the darker fabric.

Appliqué

Appliqué. Appliqué is the process of applying one piece of fabric on top of another for decorative or functional purposes.

Making Templates. Most appliqué designs given here are shown as full-size drawings for the completed designs. The drawings show dotted lines to indicate where one piece overlaps another. Other marks indicate placement of embroidery stitches for decorative purposes such as eyes, lips, flowers, etc.

For hand appliqué, trace each template onto the right side of the fabric with template right side up. Cut around shape, adding a ⅛"–¼" seam allowance.

Before the actual appliqué process begins, cut the background block. If you have a full-size drawing of the design, it might help you to draw on the background block to help with placement.

Transfer the design to a large piece of tracing paper. Place the paper on top of the design; use masking tape to hold in place. Trace design onto paper.

If you don't have a light box, tape the pattern on a window; center the background block on top and tape in place. Trace the design onto the background block with a water-erasable marker or light lead or chalk pencil. This drawing will mark exactly where the fabric pieces should be placed on the background block.

Hand Appliqué. Traditional hand appliqué uses a template made from the desired finished shape without seam allowance added.

After fabric is prepared, trace the desired shape onto the right side of the fabric with a water-erasable marker or light lead or chalk pencil. Leave at least ½" between design motifs when tracing to allow for the seam allowance when cutting out the shapes.

When the desired number of shapes needed has been drawn on the fabric pieces, cut out shapes leaving ⅛"–¼" all around drawn line for turning under.

Turn the shape's edges over on the drawn or stitched line. When turning in concave curves, clip to seams and baste the seam allowance over as shown in Figure 20.

Figure 20
Concave curves should be clipped before turning as shown.

During the actual appliqué process, you may be layering one shape on top of another. Where two fabrics overlap, the underneath piece does not have to be turned under or stitched down.

If possible, trim away the underneath fabric when the block is finished by carefully cutting away the background from underneath and then cutting away unnecessary layers to reduce bulk and avoid shadows from darker fabrics showing through on light fabrics.

For hand appliqué, position the fabric shapes on the background block and pin or baste them in place. Using a blind stitch or appliqué stitch, sew pieces in place with matching thread and small stitches. Start with background pieces first and work up to foreground pieces. Appliqué the pieces in place on the background in numerical order, if given, layering as necessary.

Machine Appliqué. There are several products available to help make the machine-appliqué process easier and faster.

Fusible transfer web is a commercial product similar to iron-on interfacings except it has two sticky sides. It is used to adhere appliqué shapes to the background with heat. Paper is adhered to one side of the web.

To use, reverse pattern and draw shapes onto the paper side of the web; cut, leaving a margin around each shape. Place on the wrong side of the chosen fabric; fuse in place referring to the manufacturer's instructions. Cut out shapes on the drawn line. Peel off the paper and fuse in place on the background fabric. Transfer any detail lines to the fabric shapes. This process adds a little bulk or stiffness to the appliquéd shape and makes hand-quilting through the layers difficult.

For successful machine appliqué a tear-off stabilizer is recommended. This product is placed under the background fabric while machine appliqué is being done. It is torn away when the work is finished. This kind of stabilizer keeps the background fabric from pulling during the machine-appliqué process.

During the actual machine-appliqué process, you will be layering one shape on top of another. Where two fabrics overlap, the underneath piece does not have to be turned under or stitched down.

Thread the top of the machine with thread to match the fabric patches or with threads that coordinate or contrast with fabrics. Rayon thread is a good choice when a sheen is desired on the finished appliqué stitches. Do not use rayon thread in the bobbin; use all-purpose thread.

When all machine work is complete, remove stabilizer from the back referring to the manufacturer's instructions.

Putting It All Together

Finishing the Top
Settings. Most quilts are made by sewing individual blocks together in rows that, when joined, create a design. There are several other methods used to join blocks. Sometimes the setting choice is determined by the block's design. For example, a House block should be placed upright on a quilt, not sideways or upside down.

Plain blocks can be alternated with pieced or appliquéd blocks in a straight set. Making a quilt using plain blocks saves time;

General Instructions

half the number of pieced or appliquéd blocks are needed to make the same-size quilt as shown in Figure 1.

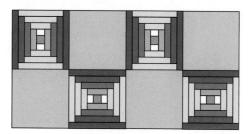

Figure 1
Alternate plain blocks with pieced blocks to save time.

Adding Borders. Borders are an integral part of the quilt and should complement the colors and designs used in the quilt center. Borders frame a quilt just like a mat and frame do a picture.

If fabric strips are added for borders, they may be mitered or butted at the corners as shown in Figures 2 and 3. To determine the size for butted border strips, measure across the center of the completed quilt top from one side raw edge to the other side raw edge. This measurement will include a ¼" seam allowance.

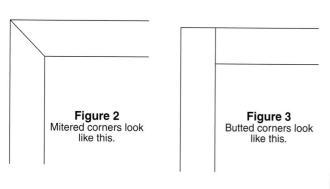

Figure 2
Mitered corners look
like this.

Figure 3
Butted corners look
like this.

Cut two border strips that length by the chosen width of the border. Sew these strips to the top and bottom of the pieced center referring to Figure 4. Press the seam allowance toward the border strips.

Measure across the completed quilt top at the center, from top raw edge to bottom raw edge, including the two border strips

already added. Cut two border strips that length by the chosen width of the border. Sew a strip to each of the two remaining sides as shown in Figure 4. Press the seams toward the border strips.

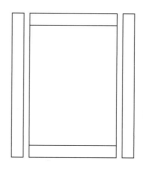

Figure 4
Sew border strips to
opposite sides; sew
remaining 2 strips to
remaining sides to make
butted corners.

To make mitered corners, measure the quilt as before. To this add twice the width of the border and ½" for seam allowances to determine the length of the strips. Repeat for opposite sides. Sew on each strip, stopping stitching ¼" from corner, leaving the remainder of the strip dangling.

Press corners at a 45-degree angle to form a crease. Stitch from the inside quilt corner to the outside on the creased line. Trim excess away after stitching and press mitered seams open (Figures 5–7).

Carefully press the entire piece, including the pieced center. Avoid pulling and stretching while pressing, which would distort shapes.

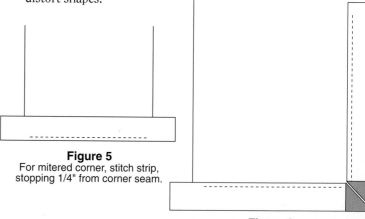

Figure 5
For mitered corner, stitch strip,
stopping 1/4" from corner seam.

Figure 6
Fold and press corner to make a
45-degree angle.

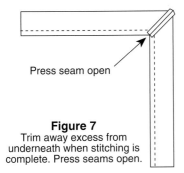

Press seam open

Figure 7
Trim away excess from underneath when stitching is complete. Press seams open.

Getting Ready to Quilt

Choosing a Quilting Design. If you choose to hand- or machine-quilt your finished top, you will need to select a design for quilting.

There are several types of quilting designs, some of which may not have to be marked. The easiest of the unmarked designs is in-the-ditch quilting. Here the quilting stitches are placed in the valley created by the seams joining two pieces together or next to the edge of an appliqué design. There is no need to mark a top for in-the-ditch quilting. Machine quilters choose this option because the stitches are not as obvious on the finished quilt. (Figure 8).

Outline-quilting ¼" or more away from seams or appliqué shapes is another no-mark alternative (Figure 9) that prevents having to sew through the layers made by seams, thus making stitching easier.

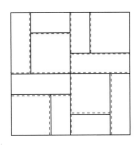

Figure 8
In-the-ditch quilting is done in the seam that joins 2 pieces.

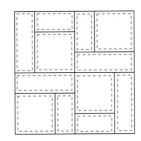

Figure 9
Outline-quilting 1/4" away from seam is a popular choice for quilting.

If you are not comfortable eyeballing the ¼" (or other distance), masking tape is available in different widths and is helpful to place on straight-edge designs to mark the quilting line. If using masking tape, place the tape right up against the seam and quilt close to the other edge.

Meander or free-motion quilting by machine fills in open spaces and doesn't require marking. It is fun and easy to stitch as shown in Figure 10.

Marking the Top for Quilting. If you choose a fancy or allover design for quilting, you will need to transfer the design to your quilt top before layering with the backing and batting. You may use a sharp medium-lead or silver pencil on light background fabrics. Test the pencil marks to guarantee that they will wash out of your quilt top when quilting is complete; or be sure your quilting stitches cover the pencil marks. Mechanical pencils with very fine points may be used successfully to mark quilts.

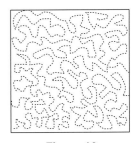

Figure 10
Machine meander quilting fills in large spaces.

Manufactured quilt-design templates are available in many designs and sizes and are cut out of a durable plastic template material that is easy to use.

To make a permanent quilt-design template, choose a template material on which to transfer the design. See-through plastic is the best as it will let you place the design while allowing you to see where it is in relation to your quilt design without moving it. Place the design on the quilt top where you want it and trace around it with your marking tool. Pick up the quilting template and place again; repeat marking.

No matter what marking method you use, remember—the marked lines should never show on the finished quilt. When the top is marked, it is ready for layering.

Preparing the Quilt Backing. The quilt backing is a very important feature of your quilt. The materials listed for each quilt in this book includes the size requirements for the backing, not the yardage needed. Exceptions to this are when the backing fabric is also used on the quilt top and yardage is given for that fabric.

A backing is generally cut at least 4" larger than the quilt top or 2" larger on all sides. For a 64" x 78" finished quilt, the backing would need to be at least 68" x 82".

To avoid having the seam across the center of the quilt

General Instructions

backing, cut or tear one of the right-length pieces in half and sew half to each side of the second piece as shown in Figure 11.

Quilts that need a backing more than 88" wide may be pieced in horizontal pieces as shown in Figure 12.

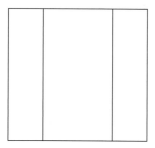

Figure 11
Center 1 backing piece with a piece on each side.

Figure 12
Horizontal seams may be used on backing pieces.

Layering the Quilt Sandwich. Layering the quilt top with the batting and backing is time-consuming. Open the batting several days before you need it and place over a bed or flat on the floor to help flatten the creases caused from its being folded up in the bag for so long.

Iron the backing piece, folding in half both vertically and horizontally and pressing to mark centers.

If you will not be quilting on a frame, place the backing right side down on a clean floor or table. Start in the center and push any wrinkles or bunches flat. Use masking tape to tape the edges to the floor or large clips to hold the backing to the

edges of the table. The backing should be taut.

Place the batting on top of the backing, matching centers using fold lines as guides; flatten out any wrinkles. Trim the batting to the same size as the backing.

Fold the quilt top in half lengthwise and place on top of the batting, wrong side against the batting, matching centers. Unfold quilt and, working from the center to the outside edges, smooth out any wrinkles or lumps.

To hold the quilt layers together for quilting, baste by hand or use safety pins. If basting by hand, thread a long thin needle with a long piece of unknotted white or off-white thread. Starting in the center and leaving a long tail, make 4"–6" stitches toward the outside edge of the quilt top, smoothing as you baste. Start at the center again and work toward the outside as shown in Figure 13.

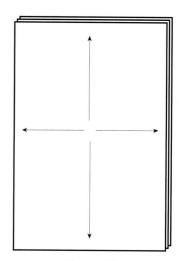

Figure 13
Baste from the center to the outside edges.

If quilting by machine, you may prefer to use safety pins for holding your fabric sandwich together. Start in the center of the quilt and pin to the outside, leaving pins open until all are placed. When you are satisfied that all layers are smooth, close the pins.

Quilting

Hand Quilting. Hand quilting is the process of placing stitches through the quilt top, batting and backing to hold them together. While it is a functional process, it also adds beauty and loft to the finished quilt.

To begin, thread a sharp between needle with an 18" piece of quilting thread. Tie a small knot in the end of the thread. Position the needle about ½" to 1" away from the starting point on quilt top. Sink the needle through the top into the batting layer but not through the backing. Pull the needle up at the starting point of the quilting design. Pull the needle and thread until the knot sinks through the top into the batting (Figure 14).

Some stitchers like to take a backstitch here at the beginning while others prefer to begin the first stitch here. Take small, even running stitches along the marked quilting line (Figure 15). Keep one hand positioned underneath to feel the needle go all the way through to the backing.

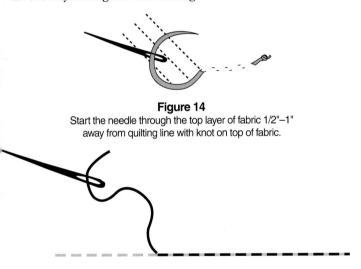

Figure 14
Start the needle through the top layer of fabric 1/2"–1"
away from quilting line with knot on top of fabric.

Figure 15
Make small, even running stitches on marked quilting line.

When you have nearly run out of thread, wind the thread around the needle several times to make a small knot and pull it close to the fabric. Insert the needle into the fabric on the quilting line and come out with the needle ½" to 1" away, pulling the knot into the fabric layers the same as when you started. Pull and cut thread close to fabric. The end should disappear inside after cutting. Some quilters prefer to take a backstitch with a loop through it for a knot to end.

Machine Quilting. Successful machine quilting requires practice and a good relationship with your sewing machine.

Prepare the quilt for machine quilting in the same way as for hand quilting. Use safety pins to hold the layers together instead of basting with thread.

Presser-foot quilting is best used for straight-line quilting because the presser bar lever does not need to be continually lifted.

Set the machine on a longer stitch length (3.0 or 8–10 stitches to the inch). Too tight a stitch causes puckering and fabric tucks, either on the quilt top or backing. An even-feed or walking foot helps to eliminate the tucks and puckering by feeding the upper and lower layers through the machine evenly. Before you begin, loosen the amount of pressure on the presser foot.

Special machine-quilting needles work best to penetrate the three layers in your quilt.

Decide on a design. Quilting in the ditch is not quite as visible, but if you quilt with the feed dogs engaged, it means turning the quilt frequently. It is not easy to fit a rolled-up quilt through the small opening on the sewing machine head.

Meander quilting is the easiest way to machine-quilt—and it is fun. Meander quilting is done using an appliqué or darning foot with the feed dogs dropped. It is sort of like scribbling. Simply move the quilt top around under the foot and make stitches in a random pattern to fill the space. The same method may be used to outline a quilt design. The trick is the same as in hand quilting; you are striving for stitches of uniform size. Your hands are in complete control of the design.

If machine quilting is of interest to you, there are several very good books available at quilt shops that will help you become a successful machine quilter.

Finishing the Edges

After your quilt is tied or quilted, the edges need to be finished. Decide how you want the edges of your quilt finished before layering the backing and batting with the quilt top.

Without Binding—Self-Finish. There is one way to eliminate adding an edge finish. This is done before quilting. Place the batting on a flat surface. Place the pieced top right side up on the batting. Place the backing right sides together with the pieced top. Pin and/or baste the layers together to hold flat referring to Layering the Quilt Sandwich.

General Instructions

Begin stitching in the center of one side using a ¼" seam allowance, reversing at the beginning and end of the seam. Continue stitching all around and back to the beginning side. Leave a 12" or larger opening. Clip corners to reduce excess. Turn right side out through the opening. Slipstitch the opening closed by hand. The quilt may now be quilted by hand or machine.

The disadvantage to this method is that once the edges are sewn in, any creases or wrinkles that might form during the quilting process cannot be flattened out. Tying is the preferred method for finishing a quilt constructed using this method.

Bringing the backing fabric to the front is another way to finish the quilt's edge without binding. To accomplish this, complete the quilt as for hand or machine quilting. Trim the batting only even with the front. Trim the backing 1" larger than the completed top all around.

Turn the backing edge in ½" and then turn over to the front along edge of batting. The folded edge may be machine-stitched close to the edge through all layers, or blind-stitched in place to finish.

The front may be turned to the back. If using this method, a wider front border is needed. The backing and batting are trimmed 1" smaller than the top and the top edge is turned under ½" and then turned to the back and stitched in place.

One more method of self-finish may be used. The top and backing may be stitched together by hand at the edge. To accomplish this, all quilting must be stopped ½" from the quilt-top edge. The top and backing of the quilt are trimmed even and the batting is trimmed to ¼"–½" smaller. The edges of the top and backing are turned in ¼"–½" and blind-stitched together at the very edge.

These methods do not require the use of extra fabric and save time in preparation of binding strips; they are not as durable as an added binding.

Binding. The technique of adding extra fabric at the edges of the quilt is called binding. The binding encloses the edges and adds an extra layer of fabric for durability.

To prepare the quilt for the addition of the binding, trim the batting and backing layers flush with the top of the quilt using a rotary cutter and ruler or shears. Using a walking-foot attachment (sometimes called an even-feed foot attachment), machine-baste the three layers together all around approximately ⅛" from the cut edge.

The materials listed for each quilt in this book often includes a number of yards of self-made or purchased binding. Bias binding may be purchased in packages and in many colors. The advantage to self-made binding is that you can use fabrics from your quilt to coordinate colors. Double-fold, straight-grain binding and double-fold, bias-grain binding are two of the most commonly used types of binding.

Double-fold, straight-grain binding is used on smaller projects with right-angle corners. Double-fold, bias-grain binding is best suited for bed-size quilts or quilts with rounded corners.

To make double-fold, straight-grain binding, cut 2¼"-wide strips of fabric across the width or down the length of the fabric totaling the perimeter of the quilt plus 10". The strips are joined as shown in Figure 16 and pressed in half wrong sides together along the length using an iron on a cotton setting with no steam.

Figure 16
Join binding strips in a
diagonal seam to eliminate
bulk as shown.

Lining up the raw edges, place the binding on the top of the quilt and begin sewing (again using the walking foot) approximately 6" from the beginning of the binding strip. Stop sewing ¼" from the first corner, leave the needle in the quilt, turn and sew diagonally to the corner as shown in Figure 17.

Fold the binding at a 45-degree angle up and away from the quilt as shown in Figure 18 and back down flush with the raw edges. Starting at the top raw edge of the quilt, begin sewing the next side as shown in Figure 19. Repeat at the next three corners.

As you approach the beginning of the binding strip, stop stitching and overlap the binding ½" from the edge; trim. Join the two ends with a ¼" seam allowance and press the seam open. Reposition the joined binding along the edge of the quilt and resume stitching to the beginning.

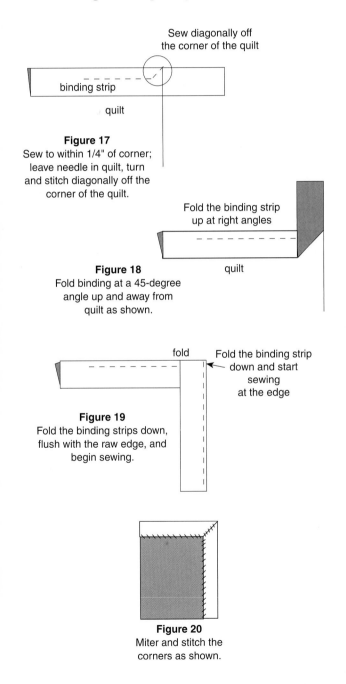

Sew diagonally off
the corner of the quilt

binding strip

quilt

Figure 17
Sew to within 1/4" of corner;
leave needle in quilt, turn
and stitch diagonally off the
corner of the quilt.

Fold the binding strip
up at right angles

quilt

Figure 18
Fold binding at a 45-degree
angle up and away from
quilt as shown.

fold

Fold the binding strip
down and start
sewing
at the edge

Figure 19
Fold the binding strips down,
flush with the raw edge, and
begin sewing.

Figure 20
Miter and stitch the
corners as shown.

To finish, bring the folded edge of the binding over the raw edges and blind-stitch the binding in place over the machine-stitching line on the backside. Hand-miter the corners on the back as shown in Figure 20.

If you are making a quilt to be used on a bed, you may want to use double-fold, bias-grain bindings because the many threads that cross each other along the fold at the edge of the quilt make it a more durable binding.

Cut 2¼"-wide bias strips from a large square of fabric. Join the strips as illustrated in Figure 16 and press the seams open. Fold the beginning end of the bias strip ¼" from the raw edge and press. Fold the joined strips in half along the long side, wrong sides together, and press with no steam (Figure 21).

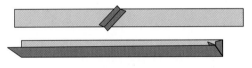

Figure 21
Fold and press strip in half.

Follow the same procedures as previously described for preparing the quilt top and sewing the binding to the quilt top. Treat the corners just as you treated them with straight-grain binding.

Since you are using bias-grain binding, you do have the option to just eliminate the corners if this option doesn't interfere with the patchwork in the quilt. Round the corners off by placing one of your dinner plates at the corner and rotary-cutting the gentle curve (Figure 22).

Figure 22
Round corners to eliminate
square-corner finishes.

As you approach the beginning of the binding strip, stop stitching and lay the end across the beginning so it will slip inside the fold. Cut the end at a 45-degree angle so the raw edges are contained inside the beginning of the strip (Figure 23). Resume stitching to the beginning. Bring the fold to the back of the quilt and hand-stitch as previously described.

Figure 23
End the binding strips as shown.

Overlapped corners are not quite as easy as rounded ones, but a bit easier than mitering. To make overlapped corners, sew binding strips to opposite sides of the quilt top. Stitch edges down to finish. Trim ends even.

Sew a strip to each remaining side, leaving 1½"–2" excess at each end. Turn quilt over and fold binding down even with previous finished edge as shown in Figure 24.

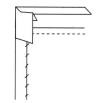

Figure 24
Fold end of binding even with
previous page.

Fold binding in toward quilt and stitch down as before, enclosing the previous bound edge in the seam as shown in Figure 25. It may be necessary to trim the folded-down section to reduce bulk.

Figure 25
An overlapped corner is not quite as
neat as a mitered corner.

Final Touches
If your quilt will be hung on the wall, a hanging sleeve is required. Other options include purchased plastic rings or fabric tabs. The best choice is a fabric sleeve, which will evenly distribute the weight of the quilt across the top edge, rather than at selected spots where tabs or rings are stitched, keep the quilt hanging straight and not damage the batting.

To make a sleeve, measure across the top of the finished quilt. Cut an 8"-wide piece of muslin equal to that length—you may need to seam several muslin strips together to make the required length.

Fold in ¼" on each end of the muslin strip and press. Fold again and stitch to hold. Fold the muslin strip lengthwise with right sides together. Sew along the long side to make a tube. Turn the tube right side out; press with seam at bottom or centered on the back.

Hand-stitch the tube along the top of the quilt and the bottom of the tube to the quilt back making sure the quilt lies flat. Stitches should not go through to the front of the quilt and don't need to be too close together as shown in Figure 26.

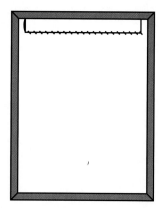

Figure 26
Sew a sleeve to the top back of the quilt.

Slip a wooden dowel or long curtain rod through the sleeve to hang.

When the quilt is finally complete, it should be signed and dated. Use a permanent pen on the back of the quilt. Other methods include cross-stitching your name and date on the front or back or making a permanent label which may be stitched to the back.